Ultimate
First
Encyclopedia

Editors: Julie Ferris, Samantha Armstrong, Sue Barraclough, Tara Benson, Charlotte Evans, Debbie Fox, Jenny Vaughn

Cover design: Mike Buckley

Designers: Ana Baillarguet, Kelly Flynn, Steven Laurie, Siân Williams

Art editors: Sue Aldworth, David Noon, Val Wright

U.S. editor: Aimee Johnson

Proofreaders: Jane Birch, Jill Somerscales, Nikky Twyman

Photography: Nick Goodall, Lyndon Parker, Tim Ridley, Andy Teare
Prop organizers: Michelle Callan, Sarah Wilson

DTP operators: Primrose Burton, Tracey McNerney

Picture research: Veneta Bullen, Nic Dean, Image Select

Artwork archivist: Wendy Allison
Assistant artwork archivist: Steve Robinson

Production Manager: Sue Wilmot
Production controllers: Richard Waterhouse, Caroline Jackson
U.S. production manager: Oonagh Phelan

Writers: Anne Civardi, John Farndon, Anita Ganeri, Jon Kirkwood, Chris Oxlade, Ruth Thomson

Index: Sylvia Potter

Consultants: John and Sue Becklake, Michael Chinery, Andrew Kemp, Keith Lye, Peter Mellett, James Muirden, Dr. Elizabeth McCall Smith, Ton Schiele, Julia Stanton, Toby Stark, Philip Steele, Dr. David Unwin

KINGFISHER
Larousse Kingfisher Chambers Inc.
95 Madison Avenue
New York, New York 10016

This edition first published by Kingfisher in 1998

Material previously published in the United States in the *First Encyclopedia*, the *First Science Encyclopedia*, and the *First Animal Encyclopedia*.

Material from *First Animal Encyclopedia* produced for Kingfisher by Warrender Grant Publications Ltd.

2 4 6 8 10 9 7 5 3 1
1(RF)(BDR)/0799/TWP/–(MAR)/115GMA

CIP data has been applied for.

ISBN 0-7534-5278-2
Printed in Singapore

Ultimate
First
Encyclopedia

KINGfISHER

NEW YORK

Contents

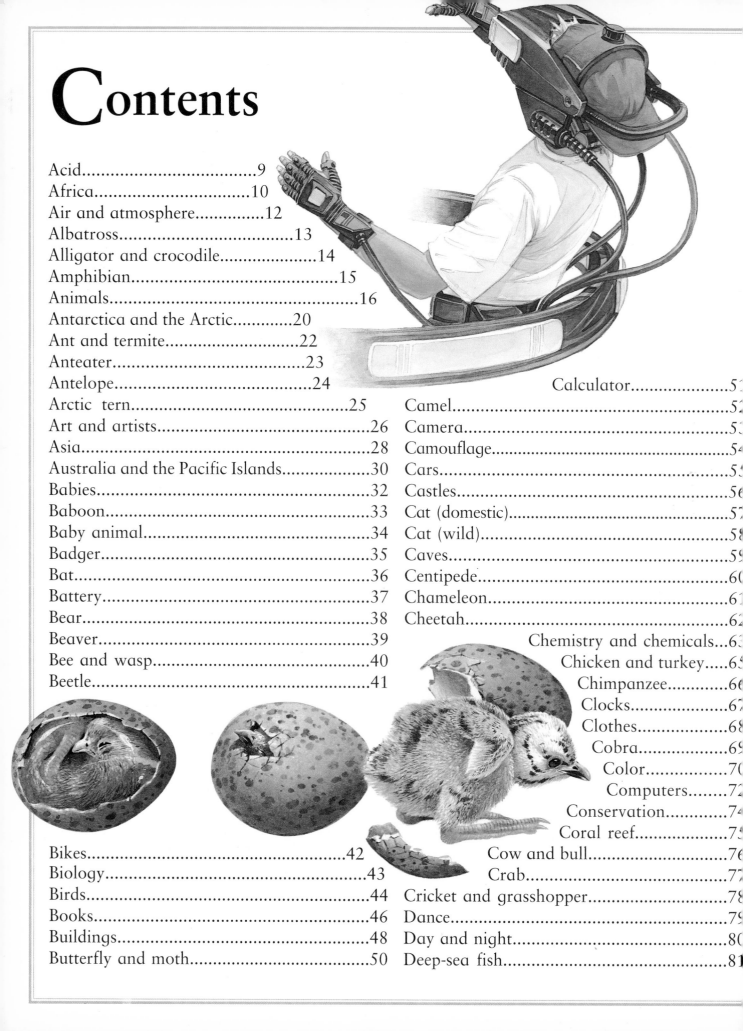

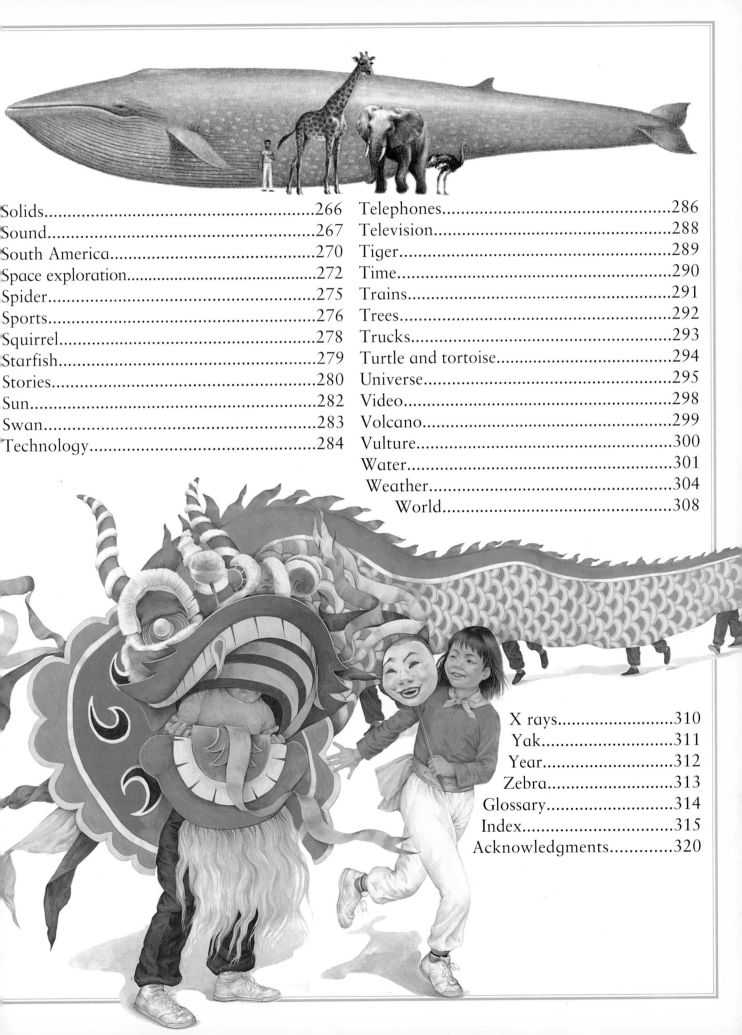

Your book

Your *Ultimate First Encyclopedia* is packed with exciting information, amazing facts, and colorful pictures. All your favorite topics appear in alphabetical order. This page will show you how to use your book.

◁ Information is written above, below, or next to each picture. Use the arrows to find out which picture to look at.

▷ Look for the numbered pictures. The numbers will help you to look at the pictures in the right order.

1  **2**  **3**

viewfinder
(you look through this)

shutter release button

Fact box

• These boxes contain extra information, facts, and figures.

film

shutter

◁ Some pictures show things that have many different parts, such as this camera. Labels show you what each part is called.

lens

Find out more

If you want to find out more about each topic, look at this box. It will tell you which pages to look at.

◁ This little person is telling you to move on to the next page.

This sign means
**DANGER!
TAKE CARE!**

Acid

Acids are chemicals. Many fruits contain acids. Vinegar and lemon juice are acids, too. These are weak acids. They make things taste sour.

Some acids are strong and can eat away at things. They are dangerous because they burn. But they can be useful. For example, some strong acids are used in making plastics. You have strong acids in your stomach to help you digest your food.

△ 1 You can find out if a substance is an acid. Ask an adult to chop some red cabbage and put it into hot water. Let it cool, then pour the liquid into clean glasses.

▷ Lemons contain an acid called citric acid. This gives the lemon its sharp taste.

 Strong acids can burn. They are dangerous.

△ 2 To test a substance, mix it with some of the cabbage water. Acids turn the cabbage water red. What happens when you test lemon juice? Now try baking soda. This is an alkali, which means it is the opposite of an acid. Alkalis turn the cabbage water green.

◁ These trees have been killed by acid rain. Acid rain forms when gases made by burning fuels, such as coal, mix with drops of water in the air. This makes a weak acid, which harms plants and eats away rocks and buildings.

Find out more
Air and Atmosphere
Chemistry and Chemicals
Fuels

Africa

Africa is the second largest and the warmest continent in the world. It has hot deserts, thick rain forests, and flat grasslands where many animals live. Many different peoples live in Africa. Most Africans live in the countryside and are farmers, but more and more are moving to the cities to find work.

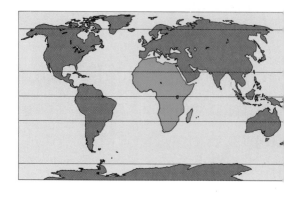

△ On this map, Africa is shown in red. Africa is joined to Asia, and the Mediterranean Sea separates it from Europe.

▽ This man sells water to thirsty people who pass by. Water is very valuable in the desert.

◁ The Sahara covers nearly one-third of Africa. It is the world's biggest desert. It has the highest sand dunes in the world.

△ Cairo is the capital city of Egypt. It is also the largest city in Africa. It is located on the edge of the desert.

▷ In many villages, women share the work of preparing meals together. Here they are pounding grain into flour to make pancakes.

▷ Diamonds from the country of South Africa are found by miners who dig thousands of feet under the ground to get them.

▷ This beautiful bottle is made out of a gourd, a plant like a pumpkin. It was made in Kenya and has a stopper shaped like a human head.

▷ Africa's large grasslands are home to many animals, like these elephants. People now use the grasslands for their herds of cattle, too.

△ Maputo is the capital city of Mozambique in southeast Africa. It is a modern city with many skyscrapers. It is also a busy port.

Find out more
Art and artists
Grasslands
History
Water
World

Air and Atmosphere

You cannot see air, but you can feel it when the wind blows. Air is a mixture of different gases. The main ones are nitrogen and oxygen. There is a blanket of air all around the Earth, called the atmosphere.

thermosphere

mesosphere

stratosphere

troposphere

meteor shower

△ The air in the atmosphere gets thinner the farther it gets from the Earth's surface. Each layer has a name.

▽ When we breathe, we take in air. Our bodies need the oxygen in the air to stay alive. We breathe out carbon dioxide as waste. Plants take in carbon dioxide, which they need to make food. They give out oxygen as waste.

△▷ This experiment shows that air has weight. The items you will need are shown above. Tape a balloon to each end of a stick. Lay a pencil between two cans and balance the stick across it. Mark the stick where it crosses the pencil. Now blow up one of the balloons. Tape it back in place, making sure that the mark on the stick is still over the pencil. Do you know why the stick doesn't balance?

Fact box
• A layer of ozone gas in the atmosphere protects living things from the Sun's harmful rays.
• The air in a bedroom weighs about the same as you do.

Find out more
Earth
Gases
Living things
Weather

Albatross

Albatrosses are the biggest of all seabirds. They live in the cold Southern Hemisphere, where they survive on fish and seawater. Albatrosses can glide for great distances on their huge wings, and are able to fly 10,000 miles in a single trip over the ocean.

△ The albatross has the longest wings of any bird—nearly 13 feet from tip to tip. It often flies without flapping its wings at all. Instead, it skims close to the waves and uses the wind to help it along.

▽ Albatrosses only return to land to raise their young. When the young birds are ten months old, they leave the island where they were born and stay at sea for several years.

Fact box
• Albatross eggs take 80 days to hatch—longer than any other species of bird.
• To feed, albatrosses settle on the ocean and catch squid.
• An albatross can travel as far as 500 miles in just 12 hours.

Find out more
Bird
Gull
Penguin
Puffin
Seabird

Alligator and Crocodile

Alligators and crocodiles are large reptiles that live in rivers and swamps in tropical areas. They float beneath the surface of the water, with only their eyes and nostrils showing, ready to snap up fish, turtles, and even big mammals in their huge jaws.

△ Crocodiles are cold-blooded creatures. They spend some of their time in the water, keeping cool and hunting. Crocodiles also spend time sunbathing on the riverbank, where they can absorb enough heat to keep active.

◁▽ The American alligator (left) has a broader and shorter jaw than the crocodile (below). Both alligators and crocodiles have between 60 and 80 teeth in their powerful jaws. They use the teeth to rip their prey to pieces.

Fact box

- Crocodiles have existed for over 200 million years.
- Alligators can grow up to 20 feet long.
- The largest, the saltwater crocodile, grows to almost 27 feet.

▽ Alligators and crocodiles lay up to 90 eggs in a nest on the riverbank made from mud and leaves. When the young hatch, they call to their mother, she digs them out, picks them up gently in her mouth, and carries them down to the water.

Find out more
Lizard

Amphibian

Amphibians are animals that live both in the water and on the land. Frogs, toads, newts, and caecilians are all amphibians. They are found everywhere except Antarctica, particularly in warm places.

△ Newts have long tails and four short legs, and they look like lizards. However, they do not have scales and their skin is moist.

△ Adult frogs and toads have four legs and no tail. Some frogs inflate their throats to make a loud croak. This helps them attract a mate.

▷ Caecilians have no legs and are similar to worms. They live underground in tropical places. Unlike most amphibians, the female caecilian guards her eggs.

◁ 1 A homemade minipond is a great way of attracting frogs and newts to your backyard. You will need a plastic bowl, some sand, pondweed, and a few stones and rocks.

◁ 2 Dig a hole in a corner of your yard and drop the bowl into it. Cover the bottom with the sand and stones, making sure that some of the rocks rise above the surface of the water. Add the pondweed, then fill the bowl with water. Over the next few weeks, watch to see if your pond has any visitors.

Find out more
Fish
Frog and Toad
Lizard
Reproduction

Animals

Animals are living things that get their energy to move and grow by eating food. They are all shapes and sizes—from huge whales to animals so tiny that thousands would fit on a teaspoon. Some animals even live inside other animals and plants. Animals can be found all over the world—in hot, dry deserts, in icy oceans, and on freezing cold mountaintops.

△ This animal is so small that it can be seen only through a microscope.

Fact box

• There are about one and a half million different kinds of animals in the world.

• The two main groups of animals are vertebrates and invertebrates. A vertebrate has a backbone. An invertebrate does not.

• Some animals eat meat, some eat plants. Some animals eat meat and plants.

▽ Blue whales are the biggest animals that ever lived on Earth. Adult blue whales are larger than any of the dinosaurs were.

blue whales

polar bear

△ Bands of colored light often appear in the night skies of the Antarctic and the Arctic. In the Arctic they are called the aurora borealis, or the northern lights. In Antarctica, they are called the aurora australis, or the southern lights.

△ The polar bear lives in the Arctic. It is a strong swimmer and good runner. It catches seals, fish, and birds with its strong paws and has a thick coat of hair to protect it against the cold.

△ Many scientists work in the Arctic and Antarctica. They record the weather, measure the depth of the ice, and study the wildlife.

△ During the winter in the Arctic and Antarctica there are only a few hours of daylight. In the summer, the opposite happens and the Sun shines all night and day.

Find out more
World

Ant and Termite

Ants and termites live in enormous nests called colonies. Inside most nests there is a queen who lays eggs, and thousands of workers who run the colony and feed her. Each worker has a job to do—some act as soldiers, guarding the nest, others gather food, and cleaners keep it tidy.

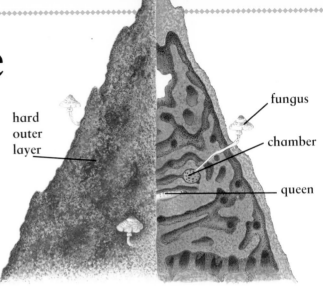

hard outer layer

fungus

chamber

queen

△ In grassland areas, termites build castles of mud that are 23 feet tall. Most termites feed on plants, but some live off a fungus that grows in their nests.

▽ A fungus grows in the nests of leafcutter ants. The ants take bits of leaf to the fungus, which "eats" the leaf and gives off sugars for the ants to eat.

king

queen

worker

soldier

◁ The queen of a termite nest lays 30,000 eggs a day. She can be 4 inches long. The king can grow to almost an inch, and the soldiers and workers are about half as big.

▷ Army ants march in vast swarms that can be 40 feet wide. They prey on insects and small animals. The worker ants take the prey back to the nest while the soldier ants stand guard. Termites are sometimes called white ants, but termites have softer bodies and wider waists than ants.

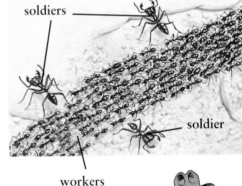

soldiers

soldier

workers

◁ Although not as tall as a termite's nest, there are lots of compartments inside an ant's nest. This is where eggs are laid and where young ants are cared for. Food is stored here, too.

Find out more
Anteater
Bee and Wasp
Insect

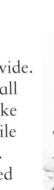

Anteater

Anteaters are mammals from South and Central America. Besides eating ants, they feed on termites and other bugs. They may look strange, but their pointy snout, sticky tongue, and sharp claws make them perfectly designed for the job of breaking into insect mounds and licking up the tasty creatures inside.

△ The collared anteater catches the termite at home in its nest, high in the trees. Using its long tail to balance itself, the anteater will suck up thousands of termites in just a few minutes.

▷ Giant anteaters shuffle along slowly, carrying their weight on the knuckles of their forefeet to keep their claws sharp for digging. In its first year, a young anteater hitches a ride on its mother's back.

◁ The collared anteater lives in trees in the rain forest. It has a prehensile (gripping) tail. It is one of only two anteaters that live off the ground. They are active at night, sleeping mainly during the day.

Find out more
Ant and Termite
Mammal
Sloth

23

Antelope

Antelope graze on the wide plains of Africa and Asia and can run fast. There are many different types of antelope. They range in size from the royal antelope, which is 10 inches tall at the shoulder, to the giant eland, which is almost 6 feet tall. Male antelope, and sometimes females, have curved horns.

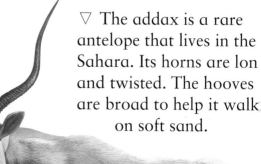

▽ The addax is a rare antelope that lives in the Sahara. Its horns are lon and twisted. The hooves are broad to help it walk on soft sand.

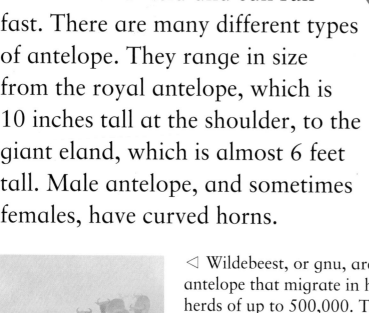

◁ Wildebeest, or gnu, are antelope that migrate in huge herds of up to 500,000. They follow the rain to find rich pastures. Wildebeest are the most common wild grazing animals in East Africa.

▷ Oryx have long, sharp horns and black-and-white faces. They live in the deserts of Arabia and Africa. Two oryx species, the Arabian and the scimitar oryx, have been hunted until there are very few left in the world.

◁ Springboks are small, graceful antelope that live on the open plains of southern Africa. These animals, which have bold markings, can be 30 inches tall. Their name comes from the way they leap, or spring, into the air.

Find out more

Camel
Deer
Llama
Reindeer
Zebra

Arctic tern

Arctic terns make the longest of all animal journeys. In the fall, after nesting on the Arctic coastline, these small seabirds fly south to spend a few months fishing on the other side of the world, in the Antarctic Ocean. In the spring, they make the long trip north again to breed.

◁ Arctic terns lay two or three eggs in nests on the frozen Arctic ground, or tundra. They defend their eggs and chicks by diving at attacking predators.

△ The Arctic tern's round trip may be more than 22,000 miles. But, by being at each pole in the summertime, it spends nearly all its life in daylight. Chicks hatch in the northern summer, and by fall they are ready to make the marathon flight south with their parents.

▽ Sooty and fairy terns are found on tropical islands. Unlike Arctic terns, they do not migrate.

sooty tern

fairy tern

Find out more
Albatross
Gull
Migration
Seabird

Art and artists

Art is something beautiful made by a person. Painting, carving, pottery, and weaving are just a few kinds of art. Artists create art for many reasons. They may want to tell a story or record an event, a person, or a place. Sometimes artists create things for a magical or religious reason, or just because they enjoy doing it.

△ The Aborigines of Australia painted rock or cave pictures thousands of years ago.

◁ The ancient Greeks painted scenes from everyday life on their pottery vases. This man is hunting deer.

▷ Everyday things can also be art. This colorful cloth was made in Ghana for clothing, but it is beautiful enough to be a work of art.

▷ Scenes from nature are popular art subjects in Japan. This beautiful print of a stormy sea was made by a Japanese artist called Hokusai.

▽ This Polynesian sculptor is carving a stone figure called a tiki. He uses a hammer and sharp chisel to carve out the image.

▷ Edgar Degas, a French artist, was very interested in showing how dancers moved. He painted many pictures of ballet dancers.

◁ The painter, Jackson Pollock, laid his canvases on the floor. Then he dripped, threw, or poured paint all over them to make swirling shapes and patterns.

Find out more
Africa
Books
Color
Stories

Asia

Asia is the biggest continent. It has large forests, deserts, and grasslands. It has many high mountains and some very long rivers. More than half the world's people live in Asia. Many are farmers. Others live in large, busy cities. Very few people live in the deserts or the rocky mountain areas.

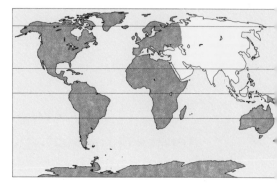

△ Asia is shown in yellow on this map. It includes nearly one-third of all the land on the Earth.

▽ Camels carry people and goods across the desert. They are also raced in the desert country of Saudi Arabia.

△ Rice is grown in the warm, wet parts of Asia. It is usually grown in fields cut into the mountainside. The low-walled fields, called terraces, are flooded with water.

◁ Kyrgyz (kir-**geez**) girls and women wear colorful clothes. Kyrgyzstan is in western Asia. The people herd sheep in the winter and farm in the summer.

◁ Shanghai is the biggest city in China. It is busy and very crowded. New skyscrapers are being built to provide homes.

△ The tea ceremony is a very old and popular tradition in Japan. The tea is made and drunk very slowly and carefully.

◁ The highest mountains in the world are in the Himalayas, between India and China. The highest of all is Mount Everest.

▽ Every July, at the full moon, richly decorated elephants parade with dancers and drummers through the streets of Kandy in Sri Lanka.

Find out more
Dance
Drama
Farming
Religion
World

Australia and the Pacific islands

Australia is a country and the world's smallest continent. Most people live in cities along the coasts. Away from the coasts the land, called the bush and the outback, is very dry and has little to eat. Australia lies between the Indian Ocean, and the South Pacific ocean—the world's largest, deepest ocean, which has many small islands. These are known as the Pacific islands.

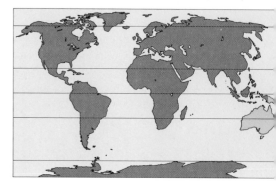
△ Australia, New Zealand, and the many islands of the Pacific Ocean are shown in orange on this map.

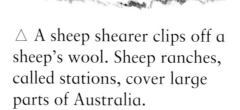
△ A sheep shearer clips off a sheep's wool. Sheep ranches, called stations, cover large parts of Australia.

▽ Many Pacific islands are surrounded by coral reefs. Many kinds of brightly colored fish live in the warm waters of the reef.

▷ These musicians are Aborigines. Their ancestors were the first people to settle in Australia, more than 45,000 years ago.

▷ Sydney is the largest city in Australia. It is also Australia's oldest city. Its world-famous Opera House (on the left of this picture) overlooks the harbor.

Uluru (Ayers Rock)

▷ The koala is a marsupial. It sleeps all day and is awake at night. It is around 2 feet (30 cm) long. It lives among the branches of eucalyptus trees and the leaves of the eucalyptus are its main food supply. Its strong claws help it to cling to tree trunks.

koala

▽ On the North Island of New Zealand there are many geysers, which are jets of boiling water and steam that burst high up into the air.

Find out more
....
Buildings
Farming
History
Stories
World

Babies

Very young children are called babies. A baby begins when a tiny egg inside its mother joins together with a tiny part of its father called a sperm. The baby grows inside its mother's uterus where it is kept safe and warm. After about nine months, the baby is ready to be born.

sperm

egg

◁ This egg is surrounded by lots of sperm. Only one of the sperm will get inside the egg.

▷ A baby grows inside its mother's uterus. It gets all the food it needs through a tube called the umbilical cord.

umbilical cord

▽ A newborn baby needs a lot of care and attention. It must be fed, bathed, kept warm, and protected.

▷ Most babies start to walk without help between the ages of 12 and 18 months.

Find out more

Food
Human body
Mammals

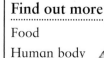

Baboon

Baboons are large monkeys that live in troops of over 100 in number. They feed on many different foods, from seeds, fruit, and grasses to small animals and eggs. They are found in Arabia and in Africa, south of the Sahara.

△ Baboons spend much of their time grooming each other. This helps form bonds between babies and mothers, and also between members of the troop. The troop is usually made up of related females, males, and one lead male.

▽ Mandrills, from the West African rain forests, are cousins of the baboon. They have bare patches on their large faces. In adult males, these are brightly colored.

▷ The gelada is a monkey similar to a baboon found in the mountains of Ethiopia, in East Africa. It has a hairless red patch in the center of its chest, from which it gets its other name —the "bleeding heart baboon." The males have very long hair over their head and shoulders.

Fact box

- Baboons sometimes weigh 88 pounds. They can be nearly 4 feet long, and have tails of 27 inches.
- Male baboons are twice as big as females.
- Baboons bark like dogs when frightened.

Find out more

Chimpanzee
Gorilla
Monkey
Orangutan

Baby animal

When they are young, many animals need care, just as human babies do. Their parents must keep them safe from harm and find food for them until they are old enough to take care of themselves.

△ When danger threatens, the male mouthbreeder fish shelters his young in his mouth. He spits them out as soon as it is safe.

△ The merganser duck sometimes gives its babies a piggyback ride. This keeps them safe until they are old enough to swim by themselves.

△ A zebra foal must learn to walk right after it is born so it can follow its mother away from danger. The male zebras will protect the herd by kicking and biting any attackers.

△ Emperor penguins keep their babies warm by carrying them on their feet.

◁ Play the baby penguin game with four or more people. Divide into two teams and stand in rows. The aim is to pass a beanbag along each row using only your feet. The first team to get the beanbag along the row wins.

Find out more

Alligator and Crocodile

Gorilla

Mammal

Penguin

Reptile

Badger

Badgers are powerful creatures, but they are also shy. They are related to skunks and, like them, have black-and-white markings. In Europe, they live in family groups in woodlands.

▽ Badgers are omnivores, which means that they eat all kinds of food. Their diet includes grasses, fruit, and nuts, as well as small animals and eggs. They are good at digging and often catch earthworms.

▽ Badgers are most active in the evening. This is when they come out to feed and to collect straw for bedding.

◁ During the day, badgers stay in underground burrows. As the group of badgers grows bigger, they dig more chambers. Some large burrows have been used for hundreds of years.

▷ Unlike the European badger, the American badger lives alone for most of the year in dry, open countryside. It also has a different face pattern.

Find out more
Mole
Skunk

Bat

Bats have big ears, furry bodies, and wings like leather. They are nocturnal mammals. This means they sleep in caves and attics during the day and fly out to feed at night.

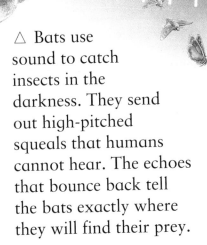

▽ Bats are the only mammals that can fly. They are very fast and acrobatic. When they chase insects, they twist and turn in midair.

△ Bats use sound to catch insects in the darkness. They send out high-pitched squeals that humans cannot hear. The echoes that bounce back tell the bats exactly where they will find their prey.

Fact box
• The "bumblebee," or hog-nosed bat may be the world's smallest mammal. It is less than an inch long.
• The South American vampire bat feeds on the blood of living animals.

▷ Flying foxes, or fruit bats, are large bats that live in tropical Africa and Asia. They eat mostly fruit. Flying foxes are important because they help spread the pollen and seeds of many plants.

Find out more
Bird
Insect
Mouse

Battery

A battery is a source of electricity. The electricity is made inside the battery by chemicals. When you turn on a flashlight, electricity flows along a wire from one end of the battery, through a bulb, and back to the battery to make the flashlight glow. After a while, the chemicals are used up and can't produce any more electricity. Then we say that the battery is dead.

△ All the machines above use batteries to work. Because the batteries inside them are small, the machines are light and portable. This makes them easy to carry around.

▽ This battery is rechargeable. This means that when it runs down the chemicals can be replaced by sending electricity through it. Most cars have battery like this to start their engines.

chemical paste

Never play with batteries or take them apart. They can be dangerous.

△ This type of battery is used in a flashlight or a radio. It is called a dry battery, because the chemicals inside it are like a dry paste.

▷ This car has an electric motor instead of a gasoline engine. The electricity for the motor comes from rechargeable batteries inside the car.

Find out more
Chemistry and Chemicals
Electricity

Bear

The bear is the largest meat-eating animal on Earth. There are many kinds of bears, and most of them live in northern parts of the world. Their thick fur coats protect them from the cold.

kodiak bear

brown bear

polar bear

black bear

△ Most bears are large and powerful, with strong claws and a good sense of smell. The Kodiak bear of Alaska is the largest of all. It weighs almost 1,800 pounds and, when standing up, can be 13 feet tall.

◁ In winter, some bears find a snug place to hibernate. Hibernation is a very deep sleep that may last many weeks. The workings of the bear' body slow down to save energy.

◁ In the fall, American black bears hunt salmon and eat berries and honey. This helps them put on the weight they need in order to survive their long hibernation.

Find out more
Mammal
Polar bear
Raccoon

38

Beaver

Beavers live near rivers in North America and northern Europe. They are great builders and use their massive front teeth to cut down trees. Beavers use these trees to make their homes, which are called lodges.

△ Beavers dam the river with branches to make a pond. In this pond they will build their lodge. Beavers use their webbed feet and big, flat tails to push themselves through the water. If alarmed, they slap their tails on the water to warn other beavers.

◁ Beaver lodges are made of sticks and mud. Beavers seal their lodges with more mud during the winter. The mud freezes hard and helps keep out predators.

▽ The adults enter the lodge by an underwater entrance and bring food to their young hidden inside. The young beavers will stay with their family for about two years. Then they leave to build their own lodges.

dam

lodge

Find out more
Mouse
Otter
Rabbit and Hare
Rat

Bee and Wasp

Bees and wasps are easy insects to spot because of their black-and-yellow, or black-and-white, striped bodies. Wasps and worker bees have a stinging tail. Bees only sting in self-defense and usually die afterward.

▽ Honeybees are ruled by a queen. They build wax rooms, called cells. **1** The queen lays an egg in each cell. **2** This grows into a larva. **3, 4** The worker bees feed it. **5, 6** Soon it grows into an adult and emerges.

△ Bees collect the sweet juice, or nectar, from flowers and use it to make honey. They keep the honey in cells to feed their growing young.

◁ The bumblebee is larger and more furry than the honeybee. It collects pollen from flowers using its hind legs. Flowers need bees to spread pollen from one flower to another. This way, the flowers can reproduce.

1

2

3

4

5

6

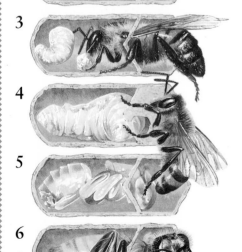

▽ Wasps are different from bees because they feed their young on insects, not honey. They use their sting to kill the insects. Adult wasps eat the sugars found in fruit, and so are attracted by the smell of sweet food or liquids.

Find out more
Ant and Termite
Fly
Insect

Beetle

There are over a quarter of a million species of beetle in the world. They come in many shapes and sizes, but all have one thing in common—a pair of delicate, folded wings protected by a hard outer casing, or shell.

△ Some species of water beetle hunt tadpoles and baby fish. Before diving, the beetles come to the surface to collect air under their wing casings.

◁ Fireflies are not flies, but flying beetles that glow in the dark. They give off light from their abdomen (rear body part) to attract mates. They let out short, regular flashes—each species has its own typical flash pattern. In some of the 1,900 species the female does not fly. She is called a glowworm.

△ Dung beetles collect a ball of dung and lay an egg in it. When the egg hatches, the new beetle larva eats the dung.

▽ Stag beetles are huge, measuring up to 3 inches long. The males often fight each other with their large jaws.

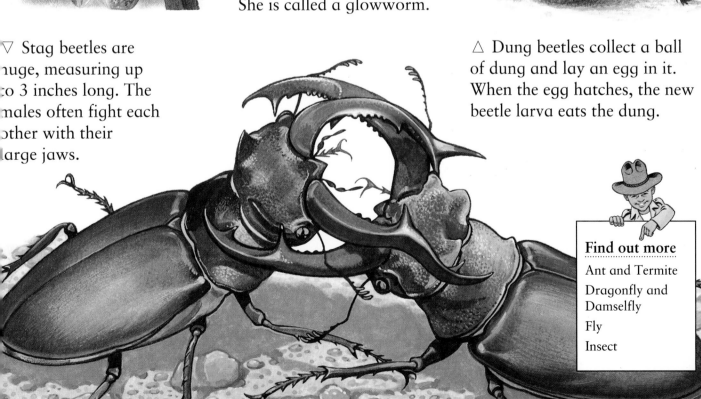

Find out more
Ant and Termite
Dragonfly and
Damselfly
Fly
Insect

Bikes

Bicycles, or bikes, and motorcycles are two-wheeled machines you can use to travel around—much faster than you can walk. Bikes are fun to ride, and because they do not have engines there is no fuel to pollute the air. Motorcycles have engines, and they can travel as fast as cars.

◁ This wooden bike was built over a hundred years ago.

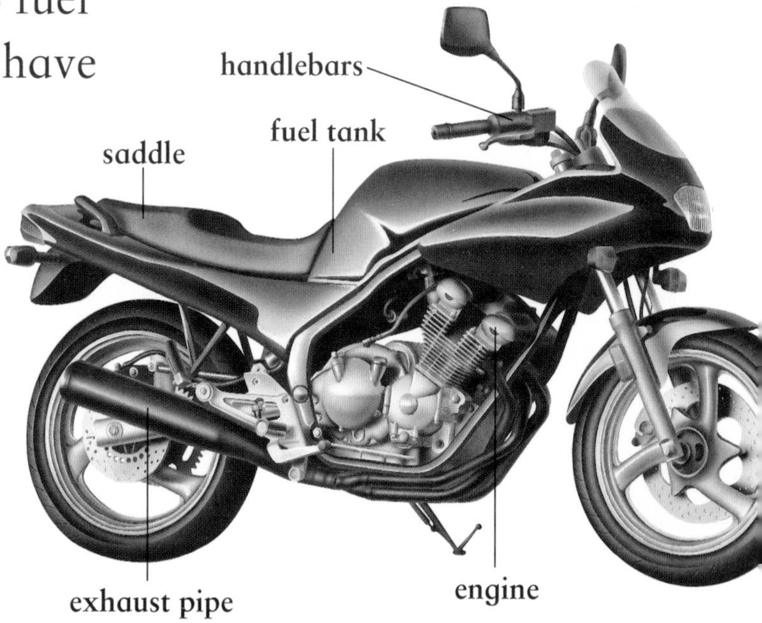

▽ To ride a bike you push the pedals. The pedals turn the chain. The chain moves the back wheel around. This makes the bike move.

handlebars

saddle

fuel tank

exhaust pipe

engine

△ The engine of a motorcycle makes the wheels go around. The engine runs on gasoline, which is stored in the fuel tank.

safety helmet

handlebars

brake lever

saddle

front reflector

back reflector

brake pad

pedal

chain

Find out more
Energy
Inventions
Machines

Famous Buildings

Leaning Tower of Pisa

Sydney Opera House

◁ The Sydney Opera House in Australia overlooks a large harbor. Its roof looks like the sails of a boat.

◁ Italy's Leaning Tower of Pisa was built on soft ground. Every year the tower leans a tiny bit more.

▷ This structure at the Epcot Center in Florida's Disney World looks like a giant golf ball.

Epcot Center

◁ Skyscrapers have a skeleton made of steel. Concrete floors, outside walls, and windows are added when the skeleton is complete.

Find out more
Australia and the Pacific islands
Castles
Religion

Butterfly and Moth

These flying insects are found worldwide, especially in warm places. Most butterflies are colorful and fly by day. Moths fly at night and are usually dull in coloring.

△ Swallowtail butterflies have tails on their wings that look like the tails of swallows.

1 egg

2 caterpillar

3 pupa

4 adult

△ **1** The female butterfly lays her eggs on a branch, and these hatch into caterpillars. **2, 3** The caterpillar eats the leaves and grows fast, until it is ready to spin itself a hard case, called a pupa. **4** Over time, it starts to change and soon becomes an adult butterfly.

▽ The death's head hawk moth of Africa gets its name from the skull-shaped pattern on its back.

◁ See for yourself how caterpillars turn into butterflies. Collect some caterpillars and put them in a large jar, along with the branches you found them on. Attach some mesh across the top with a rubber band. Add fresh leaves every day and watch the changes as they happen. Make sure you let the butterflies go as soon as they can fly.

Find out more
Bee and Wasp
Cricket and Grasshopper
Insect
Reproduction

Calculator

A calculator is a machine that adds, subtracts, multiplies, and divides. We often use electronic calculators. These can help us to work out problems with lots of numbers quickly and without making mistakes.

▽ This calculator is called an abacus. The different beads stand for different numbers. You work out the problems by sliding the beads along the wires. Calculators like this have been used for over 5,000 years.

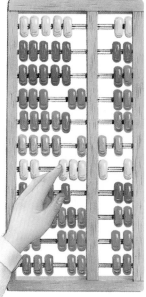

▽ The display window on a calculator shows each stage of a calculation while you are doing it. When you have finished the calculation, the answer appears in the window.

Calculator

display window

electronic circuits

keypad

battery

◁ You press the buttons on the keypad to enter the problem into the calculator.

◁ This calculator has a small battery inside it that makes the electricity it needs to work.

◁ Inside every calculator is a tiny microchip like this one. It contains very complicated electrical circuits. When electricity passes through these, they do the calculations.

Find out more
Battery
Computers
Electricity
Mathematics
Numbers

Camel

Camels live in the world's driest deserts. They have humps of fat on their backs that help them survive for days without food or water.

Fact box

• Camels can go without water for up to 17 days.
• Camels can drink 26 gallons of water at a time.
• Because they carry people and cargo across the sandy wastes, camels are known as "ships of the desert."

▽ A camel's feet are big and wide to stop it from sinking into the desert sand.

△ Camels have been used since ancient times to carry people across deserts.

△ A camel has two rows of eyelashes to shield its eyes in a sandstorm. It can also close its nostrils tight.

◁ The Arabian camel, or dromedary, has one hump. The Bactrian camel has two humps. Bactrians live in Central Asia; dromedaries live in North Africa, the Middle East, and India.

Find out more
Antelope
Cow and Bull
Giraffe
Llama

Cat (domestic)

All the domestic or house cats of today are descended from wildcats. They were first tamed over 4,000 years ago in ancient Egypt. Although domestic cats are fed by humans, they are still hunters like their ancestors, and have the same sharp teeth, pointed claws, and sensitive eyes for seeing in the dark.

tortoiseshell

blue tabby

chocolate point Siamese

▷ There are now over 40 different breeds of cat. Some, like the Siamese, have short hair. Others, like Persian cats, are longhaired.

◁ Cats make good pets because they are clean, quiet, and friendly. They can be very independent, but they still need to be well cared for. Kittens have to be trained so they get used to humans and develop good habits in the home. They enjoy human contact, especially being stroked.

▷ The African wildcat is probably the domestic cat's main ancestor, although other cats have also been taken from the wild and tamed by humans. African wildcats look like domestic tabbies, but they are slightly bigger. Their fur is also thicker and the markings are not as bold.

African wildcat   domestic cat

Find out more
Cat (wild)
Cheetah
Lion
Mammal

Cat (wild)

Except for the big cats like lions and tigers, most wild members of the cat family are fairly small. Many wild cats are hunted for their boldly patterned coats. Because of this, some are in real danger of extinction and need protection in the wild.

△ The European wildcat is found in forests from western Asia, through the continent of Europe, to Scotland. They are nocturnal animals that hunt birds and small mammals for food. The female gives birth to between three and six kittens.

▽ Caracals are cats that live in dry, scrubby areas of India and Africa. They particularly like to eat birds and will often leap up to catch them. The saying "Putting the cat among the pigeons" comes from the actions of this cat.

Fact box

- The smallest cat is the rusty-spotted cat, at just 14 inches long. It lives in India.
- The fishing cat of India has webbed paws.
- European wildcats can be 16 inches tall at the shoulder and weigh up to 22 pounds.

△ The North American bobcat gets its name from its short (bobbed) tail. It lives in forests and deserts and catches rabbits, mice, and squirrels.

Find out more

Cat (domestic)
Lion
Tiger

Caves

Caves are big holes in rock. They are usually underground, dark, and damp. Most caves are formed by water. The largest caves in the world are found in rock called limestone. Ancient humans used big dry caves to live in. Some modern people explore underground caves as a hobby. This is called caving.

bats

△ Bats often live in caves. They sleep in them during the day and fly out to hunt at night. The caves are a safe home for young bats.

stalactite column

△ Water sinks into the cracks in limestone. It eats away at the rock and makes tunnels.

△ Over thousands of years the tunnels get deeper and wider until they become big caves.

stalagmite

▷ Water dripping from the cave roof has minerals in it. When the water dries the minerals are left behind. They form stalactites and stalagmites. These can meet and form columns.

Find out more
Art
Water

Centipede

Many animals are so small that they can only be seen under a magnifying glass. We call these animals minibeasts. Minibeasts are invertebrates, which means that they have no backbone.

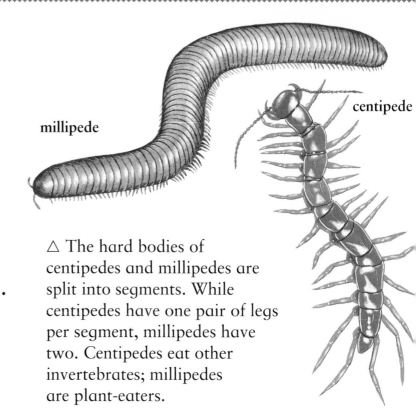

millipede

centipede

△ The hard bodies of centipedes and millipedes are split into segments. While centipedes have one pair of legs per segment, millipedes have two. Centipedes eat other invertebrates; millipedes are plant-eaters.

◁ There are many types of minibeast. Spiders are arachnids, and they have eight legs.

▷ Wood lice are land-living crustaceans, a group normally found in water.

◁ Yellow jackets are insects. They have six legs, and bodies with three sections.

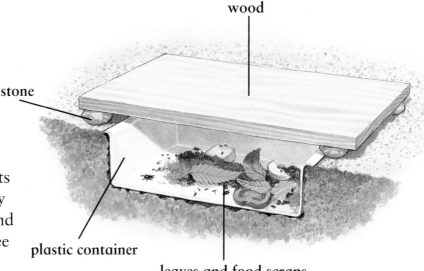

wood

stone

plastic container

leaves and food scraps

▷ Snails are mollusks that carry their shells on their backs.

◁ Worms belong to a group called the annelids. They have long, soft bodies that are divided into many segments.

△ A good way of catching minibeasts is by making a trap. Put a plastic container in a hole and add some leaves, twigs, and scraps of food. Cover it with a piece of wood supported on stones. Leave your trap overnight. How many types of minibeast did you catch?

Find out more
Bee and Wasp
Insect
Slug and Snail
Spider

Chameleon

Chameleons are unusual lizards that can change their skin color. They do this when they are angry or frightened, when the light or temperature levels change, or to hide themselves.

△ There are special cells called melanophores underneath a chameleon's skin. These can change color to match the chameleon's surroundings, making it more difficult to see.

▽ A chameleon will sit in a tree waiting to catch insects. A strong, curled tail holds it to the branch, while swiveling eyes allow it to look forward and backward at the same time. Then its long tongue darts out to catch its prey.

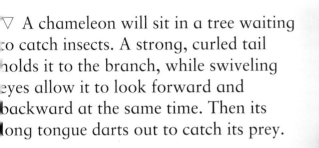

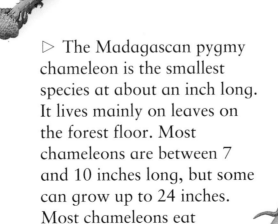

Fact box

- There are about 100 species of chameleon.
- Around 50 of these species live on the island of Madagascar.
- Chameleons usually live in trees, but come down to lay their eggs in the soil.

▷ The Madagascan pygmy chameleon is the smallest species at about an inch long. It lives mainly on leaves on the forest floor. Most chameleons are between 7 and 10 inches long, but some can grow up to 24 inches. Most chameleons eat insects, and the bigger ones also eat birds.

Find out more

Alligator and Crocodile

Cobra

Lizard

Reptile

Cheetah

Cheetahs are slim, spotted cats with long legs. They are the fastest land animals and can reach speeds of over 60 miles per hour. Cheetahs are found in the open plains of Africa, south of the Sahara.

△ Cheetahs can only run at high speed for a short distance. They bring down their prey by tripping them.

◁ Female cheetahs have up to four babies at a time. The cubs have a long coat of gray hair, which makes them look like honey badgers. Honey badgers are aggressive animals, so other animals will not go near them. This "disguise" keeps the cubs safe from harm.

Fact box
• Cheetahs are the only cats that cannot draw their claws back fully. They use them to grip while sprinting after prey.
• Cheetahs are 4.5 feet long and have tails measuring 30 inches.

▷ Cheetahs once lived in North Africa, the Middle East, and India. But they have been trapped and tamed in Asia, and are now seriously endangered. Cheetahs are also rare in Africa.

Find out more
Cat (wild)
Lion
Tiger

Chemistry and Chemicals

Chemistry is the study of what things are made from. People who study chemistry are called chemists. Chemicals are the solids, liquids, and gases that chemists use or make.

Different chemicals are useful in different ways. We use some for cleaning and others for cooking. Some are used in factories, to make plastics or paint. Farmers use chemicals to help crops to grow, and to kill weeds or insects.

carbon atom

hydrogen atom

△ Like all substances, chemicals are made up of atoms. These cling together in groups called molecules. This picture shows a model of a polyethylene molecule. It is made up of carbon and hydrogen atoms.

▷ Some chemicals seem to disappear when you put them in water. We say they dissolve. How well do salt, sugar, and flour dissolve?

sugar

salt

flour

sugar

salt

△ Sugar and salt are chemicals that look the same. Is it easy to tell them apart by tasting them?

oil

▽ Some chemicals look the same, but you can tell them apart by feeling them. Try touching lemon juice and cooking oil.

Don't touch any chemicals unless an adult says they are safe. Some are poisonous. Some can burn your skin.

lemon juice

▽ Rust is made when the metal iron combines with the gas oxygen (which is in the air). When chemicals join together to make new chemicals, we call it a chemical reaction.

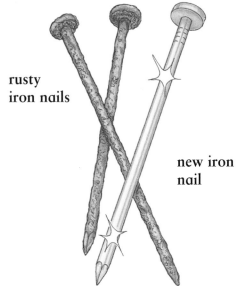

rusty iron nails

new iron nail

△ Hundreds of years ago, people called alchemists tried to make gold from other kinds of metals. This was impossible, but, as they worked, alchemists learned about what happened when they mixed different chemicals. You could say that alchemists were the first chemists.

▷ We can tell some chemicals by their smell. Slices of potato and apple look the same, but smell different.

pebble

polystyrene pebble

potato

apple

Fact box

• Chemicals can occur in very different forms. For example, graphite (found in pencils) and diamonds are both forms of the chemical carbon.

△ We can tell some chemicals apart by their weight. For example, a lump of polystyrene weighs much less than a rock of the same size.

Find out more

Acid
Fuels
Gases
Solids

Chicken and Turkey

Chickens and turkeys are kept as farm animals all over the world. They are related to wild birds that were tamed by humans over 4,000 years ago. Chickens and turkeys can fly for short distances, but they prefer to walk or run.

△ Barnyard chickens eat seeds and small insects. They will also peck grain that is sprinkled on the ground. On some big farms, however, hens are fed special food and kept in small cages.

△ Male chickens are called roosters and have large crests on their heads and a ruff of long feathers around their necks. They often make a loud crow, especially at daybreak. Female chickens are called hens. They are smaller and less colorful than roosters. Hens are kept for both their meat and their eggs.

◁ Turkeys are big birds with a fleshy red "wattle" around their necks. They come from North and Central America, and were brought to Europe in about 1519 by Spanish explorers.

Find out more
Birds
Duck and Goose
Peacock
Swan

Chimpanzee

Chimpanzees, or chimps, are our closest animal relatives, and are some of the most intelligent animals. They live in tropical rain forests and woodlands in Africa. Chimps eat fruits, leaves, and seeds, but they also like termites and ants.

△ Chimps sometimes use twigs to pry insects out of their mounds, and will crack nuts open by hitting them with stones.

Fact box

• The tallest male chimps are about 5 feet tall when they stand up— about as big as a small human adult. Female chimps are shorter.
• Chimps can live to be 60 years old.
• Chimps live in groups. These have between 15 and 80 members.

△ Chimps spend a lot of their time in trees. They use their long arms to swing from branch to branch in search of food. At night, they build nests of leaves to sleep in.

◁ Chimps usually move around on all fours, but they can also walk upright, which leaves their hands free. If attacked, a chimp may defend itself by throwing stones.

Find out more
Baboon
Gorilla
Monkey
Orangutan

Clocks

We use clocks to measure time. Inside every clock there is a special part that works at the same, regular speed. In electric clocks it is a regular electrical signal. This controls the speed at which the hands move, or how often the numbers on the display change. Some older clocks have a swinging pendulum to move the hands at a regular speed.

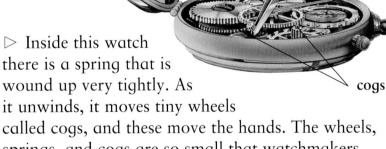

△ Clocks come in all shapes and sizes. Many are battery-powered. Some watches are "digital." This means the time is shown as numbers in a window. Other watches have a dial and hands.

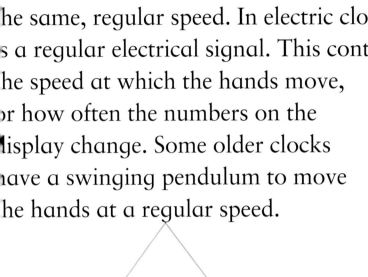

swing   swing

△ A pendulum is a weight on the end of a string or rod. Each swing of the pendulum takes exactly the same time.

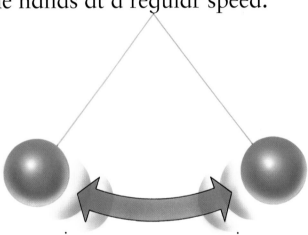

tweezers

cogs

▷ Inside this watch there is a spring that is wound up very tightly. As it unwinds, it moves tiny wheels called cogs, and these move the hands. The wheels, springs, and cogs are so small that watchmakers have to use fine tweezers to mend or move them.

◁ This old-fashioned grandfather clock has a long pendulum to control the speed of its hands.

◁ Long ago, people used sundials instead of clocks. The dial is marked in hours. The Sun shines on the pointer, which casts a shadow. This shows you the time.

Find out more
Day and Night
Energy
Machines

Clothes

Clothes are the things we wear on our bodies. People wear different clothes to suit the jobs they do, the games they play, and the weather. In some jobs people wear uniforms so that they are easy to recognize. Most clothes are made in factories.

Inuit child

◁ People who live in very cold places wear clothes that will keep them warm and dry.

Tuareg man

▷ In hot, dry deserts people wear long robes and scarves. This protects them from the heat of the Sun.

▽ When the weather is wet and rainy, waterproof things help to keep your clothes dry.

▽ Firefighters wear special clothes to protect them from heat and smoke.

speed skater

◁ Clothes for sports must be light and easy to move around in. They are often made of tight, stretchy fabric.

firefighter

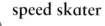

Find out more
Dance
Deserts
Drama
Space exploration
Sports

Cobra

Cobras are poisonous snakes found in Africa, India, and Asia. The most deadly cobras are the mambas of Africa. A bite from a mamba will kill unless the victim is given antivenin (an antidote to snake venom) very quickly. Many people die each year from cobra bites.

Fact box

• Cobras eat small vertebrates (creatures with backbones).
• The black mamba moves as fast as a running human.
• Cobra venom stops the heart and lungs from working.

△ The king cobra is found in areas stretching from southern China to Indonesia. Reaching 18 feet in length, it is the world's longest poisonous snake. The female king cobra lays up to 40 eggs.

▷ In India, snake charmers catch common cobras. They play a tune on a pipe and the cobra rises up from the basket to "dance."

▽ One of the cobra's main predators is the mongoose. Mongooses move very quickly and can avoid getting bitten. When frightened, the cobra rears up and spreads its hood.

Find out more

Lizard
Rattlesnake
Reptile

Color

When we see color, we see colored light. Ordinary light, such as sunlight, is called white light. It seems to have no color, but it is really a mixture of every color there is.

When we see an object, what we actually see is light bouncing off it into our eyes. Often, only a few of the colors in the light bounce off the object. A leaf looks green, for example, because only green light bounces off it.

Fact box

• The pictures in this book are made up of tiny colored dots. The colors are yellow, a kind of dark pink, a shade of blue, and black. These four colors mix together to make all the colors you see.

1

△ **1** Put a saucer on a sheet of stiff white card. Draw around it and cut out the circle.

2

△ **2** Draw lines to divide the circle into three. Color one part red, one part green, and one part blue.

3

△ **3** Push a pencil through the center of the circle. Spin it like a top. The three colors mix together, making the disk look white.

△ A rainbow happens when the Sun shines during a shower of rain. The light reflects (bounces off) the raindrops and the light breaks up into all its different colors.

▽ Red, blue, and green are called the primary colors of light because they mix together to make white light.

△ Flowers are often brightly colored. Their colors signal to insects and birds that inside there is sweet nectar, which they like to drink. This hummingbird uses its long, thin beak to reach deep inside the flower.

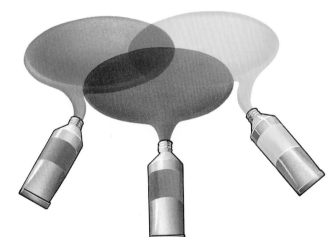

△ Red, blue, and yellow are the primary colors of paint. With these three colors you can make any color you want.

▽ The ladybug's coloring warns other animals that it is not good to eat.

▷ We use colored lights to send messages. On traffic lights, red means "stop," yellow means "take care," and green means "go."

◁ This insect is exactly the same color as the leaves it lives on. Its disguise makes it difficult for its enemies to see, and protects the insect from being eaten.

Find out more
Light and Lenses
Living things

Computers

A computer is an amazing machine. It can do calculations, store and find information. It works using microchips (very small electrical circuits) that act as its brain and memory. A computer cannot think for itself. A human being has to give it a set of instructions, called a program. These are usually stored on a disk inside the computer.

△ A CD-ROM is a disk containing information that the computer can turn into words, pictures, and sounds.

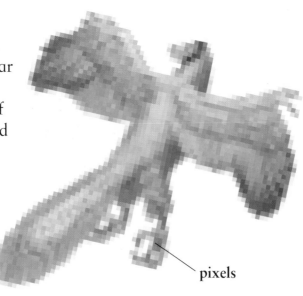

▷ The letters and pictures that appear on a computer screen are made of tiny dots of colored light called pixels. This archaeopteryx shows how pixels make up a picture.

pixels

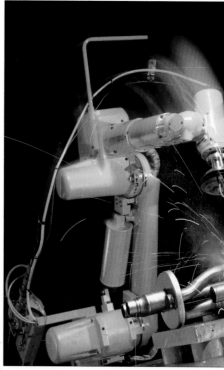

◁ You move a mouse around to point at things on the screen. A cursor on the screen follows your movements.

△ This is a robot that puts car parts together in a factory. It is controlled by a computer that has been programmed to tell the robot what to do.

72

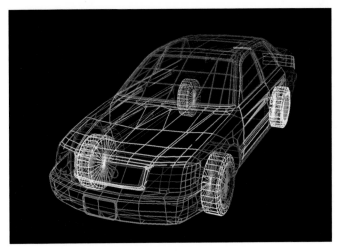

△ Engineers use computers to design cars. The picture on the screen shows what the car will look like when it is built.

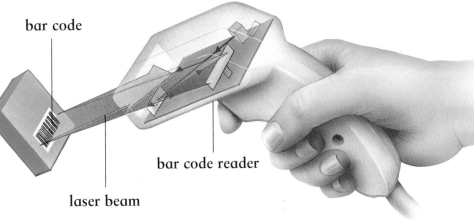

bar code

bar code reader

laser beam

◁ Bar codes are patterns of black and white stripes. They contain coded information about the objects they are printed on. A laser beam scans the bar code and sends the information to a computer. You can see an example of this in a supermarket.

◁ With a headset like this you can have the feeling of being in another world—perhaps among the dinosaurs, or in Ancient Rome. This is called virtual reality. The headset shows pictures of the world created by the computer. It also plays sounds made by the people and animals in that world.

Find out more
Calculator
Electricity
Mathematics
Numbers
Technology

Conservation

Many animals are in danger of dying out, or becoming extinct. This may be because their habitat has been destroyed or polluted, or because they have been hunted. It is important for us to conserve these animals and their homes.

△ Litter pollutes the environment. It is also dangerous to animals, who may get trapped inside empty cans and bottles. Collecting litter is an excellent way of helping animals.

△ Many corn crakes die when farmers cut their fields. New harvesting methods are now helping them survive.

◁ Dodos once lived on the island of Mauritius, but because they could not fly they were easily hunted by sailors visiting the island. In 1680, the dodo became extinct.

▽ In the last 50 years, the survival of whales has been threatened by overhunting. Nowadays, whale hunting is carefully controlled.

Find out more
Bison and
Musk ox
Panda
Tiger
Whale

Dance

ballet shoes

When you dance, you move your body in time to music. You may follow a pattern of steps, or just twist and twirl and stamp your feet to fit the music. People all over the world love to dance. Many dancers use their hands and bodies to tell a story.

◁ This Indian dancer moves her hands and fingers in a special way. Her movements tell a story about the Hindu gods.

▷ Most ballet dancers first learn to dance when they are young. They learn special positions for their hands and feet.

◁ Spanish flamenco dancers stamp and tap their heels and toes. They move their hands, while they twist and turn their bodies in time to guitar music.

▷ These Russian folk dancers jump high and kick out their legs to fast music.

Find out more
Art and artists
Asia
Europe
Music
Religion

Day and Night

Days and nights happen because the Earth spins as it travels around the Sun. The Sun shines onto the side of the Earth facing it. As the Earth spins, different parts of the Earth's surface get more or less sunlight. When the part of the Earth you live on is in the sunlight, you have day.

◁ Most people sleep at night and play or work in the day. But some animals, such as owls, sleep by day and look for food at night. They are called nocturnal.

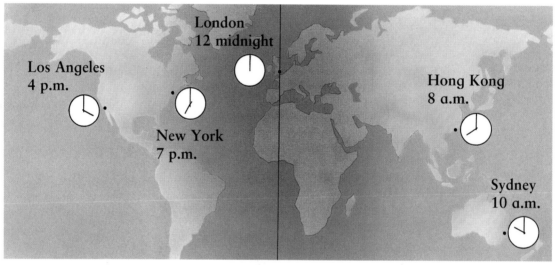

Los Angeles
4 p.m.

London
12 midnight

New York
7 p.m.

Hong Kong
8 a.m.

Sydney
10 a.m.

△ When it is day where you are, it is night on the other side of the world. The time changes as you travel around the world.

◁ Try this experiment to see how day and night happen. Work with a friend in a dark room. Shine a torch on one side of a globe. The other person turns the globe around slowly. Can you see how each part of the globe is in the light for a time, while the rest is in shadow?

Find out more
Clocks
Earth
Living things
Seasons
Solar System

Deep-sea fish

Down at the bottom of the ocean, the water is cold and dark. Food is scarce, and fish here must prey on one another or eat dead fish. Deep-sea fish are fairly small, but they often have huge, gaping jaws and stretchy stomachs to make the most of any food around.

▷ The gulper can completely unhinge its huge jaws so it can swallow larger fish. It also has a stomach that expands to deal with the largest of meals.

▽ Tubeworms called riftia live in the hot waters gushing from volcanic vents on the ocean floor. They eat bacteria that feed on sulfur from the hot vents.

Fact box

• Tripod fish stand on three long fins, waiting for their prey.
• If attacked, some deep-sea fish create flashes of light.
• Many deep-sea fish are totally blind.

▽ Like many fish in the dark depths, the anglerfish makes its own light. The female anglerfish's light dangles on a long stalklike fin in front of her mouth, to lure prey into her jaws. The male has no "fishing fin" and relies on the female to eat. He bites into her and feeds on her blood.

anglerfish

gulper eel

dragonfish

riftia

◁ Dragonfish have eyes, but they find their food in the dark by waving their long feelers through the water.

Find out more
Eel
Fish
Shark

Deer

Deer come in all shapes and sizes, from the tiny pudu to the large moose. They are graceful mammals that can run swiftly from danger. Deer are found in the Northern Hemisphere and South America.

△ **1** Make a cast of a deer hoofprint to keep forever. First take a piece of cardboard 2 or 3 inches wide and 20 inches long. Bend the cardboard into a circle around the hoofprint and fasten with tape.

△ Each year, male deer grow a new set of antlers. During the breeding season, they fight fierce battles with each other to become leader of the herd.

△ **2** Mix some plaster of Paris powder with water to make a thick paste. Pour the paste into the cardboard mold until it reaches just below the top of the cardboard.

△ **3** Leave it until it hardens, then carefully lift off the plaster in its mold. Take your cast home and remove the cardboard. Using an old toothbrush, clean off any soil from the plaster cast.

Find out more

Antelope
Elk
Mammal
Reindeer

Deserts

A desert is a dry place where little or no rain falls. Few people live there. Only tough plants and animals can live in these rocky or sandy places. Many deserts are blazing hot during the day and freezing cold at night. Some deserts are cold most of the time.

△ Monument Valley is in the states of Arizona and Utah. Strong winds blow the sand around, and this has worn the rocks into strange shapes.

▷ These people are nomads. This means that they travel around to find food and water. They often live in tents that can be moved easily.

desert scorpion

△ The scorpion is a deadly hunter. It has a poisonous stinger in its tail.

prickly pear cactus

camel

◁ A camel can travel a long way without eating and drinking. It stores fat in its hump and uses this for food.

◁ Cactus plants store water in their thick stems. The spines protect the plants from being eaten by animals.

Find out more

Africa

Antarctica and the Arctic

Asia

North America

Plants

Dinosaurs

Dinosaurs lived on Earth millions of years ago. These scaly-skinned animals were all shapes and sizes. Some were huge creatures that weighed ten times as much as an elephant, others were the size of chickens. Some were fierce meat-eaters and some ate only plants.

△ Scientists study fossils of dinosaur footprints. They can use them to work out how they moved and how fast they ran.

◁ Dinosaurs laid eggs. Maiasaura laid eggs in a nest, which she dug in the ground. She cared for her babies after they hatched.

Fact box

• The word dinosaur means terrible lizard.

• Dinosaurs lived on Earth long before the first human beings.

• Dinosaurs became extinct about 65 million years ago. We do not know why they died out.

Maiasaura
(**My**-a-saw-ra)

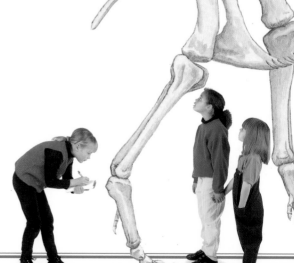

▷ This is the skeleton of Tyrannosaurus rex. It lived in North America. It was about 50 feet (15 m) long and 20 feet (6.5 m) tall. It weighed around 20 tons.

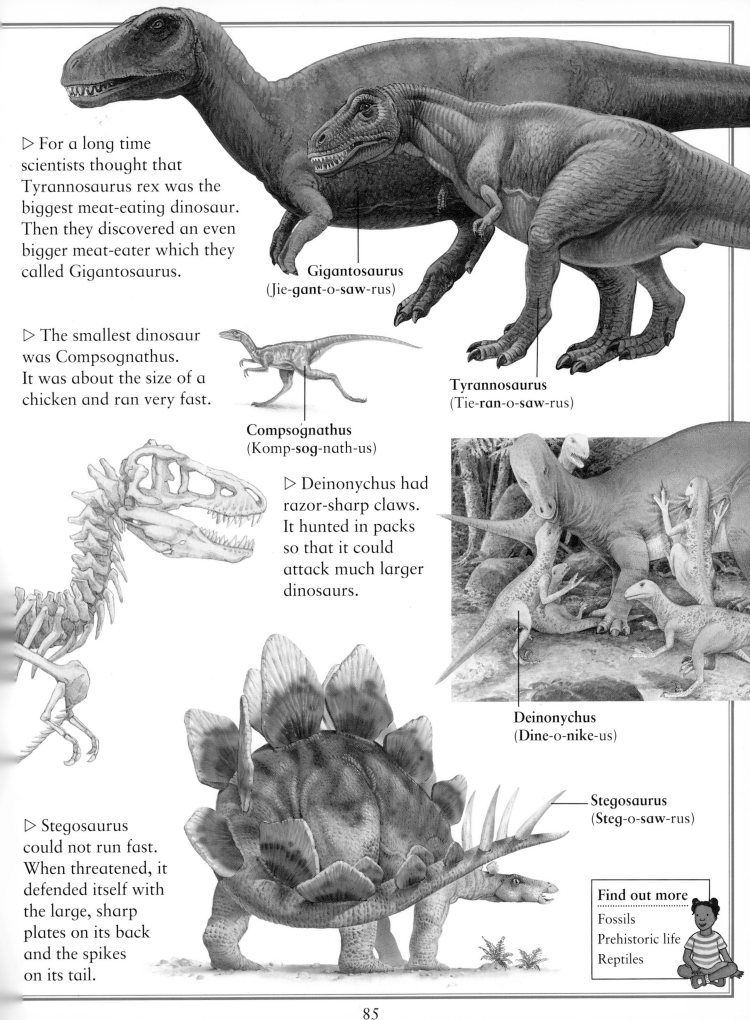

▷ For a long time scientists thought that Tyrannosaurus rex was the biggest meat-eating dinosaur. Then they discovered an even bigger meat-eater which they called Gigantosaurus.

Gigantosaurus
(Jie-**gant**-o-**saw**-rus)

Tyrannosaurus
(Tie-**ran**-o-**saw**-rus)

▷ The smallest dinosaur was Compsognathus. It was about the size of a chicken and ran very fast.

Compsognathus
(Komp-**sog**-nath-us)

▷ Deinonychus had razor-sharp claws. It hunted in packs so that it could attack much larger dinosaurs.

Deinonychus
(Dine-o-**nike**-us)

Stegosaurus
(Steg-o-**saw**-rus)

▷ Stegosaurus could not run fast. When threatened, it defended itself with the large, sharp plates on its back and the spikes on its tail.

Find out more
Fossils
Prehistoric life
Reptiles

85

Dog (domestic)

Dogs were domesticated about 12,000 years ago, when cavemen first tamed the Asiatic wolf. Since then, dogs have lived with people wherever they have traveled. Over time they have been bred to help people both in their everyday lives and in their work.

Bernese mountain dog

Labrador retriever

Yorkshire terrier

▷ There are about 400 dog breeds, which are divided into seven groups. These are: sporting dogs; hounds; working dogs; terriers; toy dogs; non-sporting dogs; and herding dogs. The Bernese mountain dog is a working dog, the Labrador retriever is a sporting dog, and the Yorkshire terrier is a toy dog.

▽▷ The collie (below) and the corgi (right) are both herding dogs. Collies help round up sheep. Corgis once helped herd cattle. Many collies work on farms, but most corgis are now just pets.

△ Dogs kept as pets should be taught to walk on a leash and housebroken. They must be properly cared for throughout their lives.

Find out more
Cat (domestic)
Dog (wild)
Fox
Hyena

Dog (wild)

In many ways wild dogs look and behave like domestic dogs, and they are related. However, wild dogs are usually afraid of humans and cannot be trained. These meat-eaters often live in packs and are found all over the world.

▷ Like most wild dogs, the Cape hunting dogs of East Africa are fierce killers. They have long front teeth for piercing or tearing, and sharp cheek teeth for slicing meat into small chunks. They work in teams to chase down antelope, zebra, and wildebeest.

◁ Wild dogs rely on their sense of smell and sharp hearing for hunting. Once they have found their prey's scent, they give chase. Like other dogs, North American coyotes (left) howl to call up the pack for a hunt.

Fact box

• The dhole of India can kill bears and even tigers.
• Golden jackals of southeastern Europe now live mostly on humans' trash.
• The coyote is sometimes called the prairie wolf.

◁ Jackals live in Africa and Asia. They hunt mainly alone at night, and form packs only when there is a chance of sharing a lion's kill.

Find out more
Dog (domestic)
Fox

Dolphin

Dolphins are intelligent, graceful sea creatures. They are not fish, but mammals and, like us, they breathe air. They make clicking sounds to help them find their way, catch their prey, and communicate.

white-sided dolphin

△ There are over 30 species of dolphin, found in seas all over the world.

Fact box

• A dolphin's top speed is 25 miles per hour.
• A dolphin breathes through a blowhole in the top of its head.

spotted dolphin

◁ Dolphins send out sounds in pulses. Then they listen for echoes reflected back from nearby objects to find out what is around them. This way, they can track down fish to eat.

▽ Bottle-nosed dolphins love to play. Like many other dolphin species, their streamlined shape and powerful tails help them speed through the water and they often jump high into the air. They live in big family groups called schools, and like to race alongside boats.

bottle-nosed dolphin

Find out more
Killer whale

Donkey

Patient and strong, donkeys are used all over the world to carry people and freight. Their small feet and thick coats equip them for working in dry, rocky places. Because they are quiet animals and are gentle with children, donkeys are often kept as pets.

▽ Donkeys range in color from almost white to nearly black. They usually have two dark stripes running along their backs and across their shoulders. Unlike horses, only the ends of their tails have long hairs.

▽ Donkeys are descended from wild asses that were tamed by the ancient Egyptians. Wild asses look very similar to donkeys, with large pointed ears and small hooves. They have thin black stripes on their legs, unlike donkeys.

▽ Donkeys are usually good workers. They can also be stubborn and will make a loud braying noise if they are angry or upset.

Find out more
Horse
Zebra

Dragonfly and Damselfly

Dragonflies are the fastest flying insects, swooping over the streams and ponds where they live at up to 55 miles per hour. Damselflies are thinner and more delicate, with a slow, fluttering flight.

▷ The wings of the damselfly are almost transparent. They shimmer as the damselfly searches for small insects to eat.

△ Dragonflies and damselflies live near water. The young, called nymphs, hatch from eggs laid on plants. They feed on other water creatures, and after two year the nymphs grow into adults.

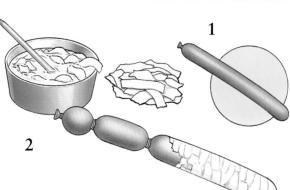

△ **1** To make a model dragonfly, start by blowing up a long balloon. **2** Twist and tie the balloon twice to make the three body sections, then cover the balloon with several layers of papier-mâché. When this is dry, paint the body.

▷ **3** Make the wings from wire bent into shape. Cover them with plastic wrap, then attach them to the body with some more wire. Attach pipe cleaners or straws to the middle section for the legs. For the eyes, cut a ping-pong ball in half and glue it to the head.

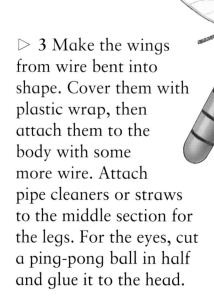

Find out more
Ant and Termite
Bee and Wasp
Beetle
Fly
Insect

Drama

Drama is a story told in words and actions. Most dramas are called plays. They are performed by actors on a stage in front of an audience. Most plays are performed in a theater. You can also watch drama on television and in the movies, or listen to it on the radio.

◁ Puppets can be used instead of people to perform plays. These puppets are from India.

▷ You could put on your own play. Decide on a story and make some scenery. Dress up in costumes and put on makeup. Then ask people to come along and watch.

△ This woman is a mime artist. She uses her body instead of words to tell a story.

◁ Kabuki is a type of play performed in Japan. All the parts are played by men. They wear colorful costumes and lots of makeup.

Find out more
History
Jobs
Stories

Duck and Goose

Ducks and geese are water birds. Members of this family live in most parts of the world. They have thick plumage (feathers) to keep them warm, and webbed feet for paddling along in water.

△ Geese are generally bigger than ducks and have longer necks. Geese have big beaks for pulling up and eating grass. Ducks have flatter beaks for sifting food from the water.

◁ Ducks have short legs, and they waddle when they walk. Their feet have three front toes in a web and a rear toe that is free. Almost all duck species live in fresh water. Besides feeding on insects and worms, they eat vegetable matter.

△ Eider ducks breed along icy northern coasts. To keep her eggs warm, the female lines the nest with fluffy feathers (down) plucked from her breast.

▽ Most Canada geese that breed in Canada and Alaska migrate to Mexico and the southern United States in the winter. When they fly, they often make a honking noise.

△ Male ducks are called drakes. They often have colorful plumage, which is designed to attract females. Female ducks are usually dull brown.

Find out more
Bird
Gull
Migration
Pelican
Swan

Eagle

Strong wings, sharp eyes, and powerful talons make eagles great hunters. Their large, hooked bills are used for slicing open and eating— not for killing. They also scavenge if they find dead animals. These big birds of prey are found in regions from the Arctic to the tropics.

◁ The golden eagle (left) and the white-tailed sea eagle are the most widespread eagle species. They are found in Europe and northern Asia. Like most eagles, they nest on cliffs, raising one or two chicks a year.

△ The North American bald eagle is the national bird of the United States. It is not really bald, but has contrasting white head and brown body feathers. It lives close to lakes, rivers, and coasts.

Fact box
• Because they are so strong, eagles have been symbols of war and national power for thousands of years.
• Eagles mate for life and return to use the same nest every year.

▷ Harpy eagles come from the jungles of South America and the South Pacific. They are powerful hunters, eating sloths, macaws, and monkeys. The great harpy eagle (right) is the largest eagle.

Find out more
Bird
Owl
Seabird
Vulture

Earth

The Earth is the planet we live on. It formed about 4.5 billion years ago from a cloud of dust, rock, and gas. Since then, volcanoes, earthquakes, wind, and rain have changed its surface. Scientists think the Earth is the only planet in the Solar System where plants and animals can live.

△ Two-thirds of the Earth is covered in salty seawater. Around the Earth is a blanket of air, called the atmosphere.

▽ The Earth is a giant ball of rock. Beneath the surface, this rock is so hot that some of it is molten (melted) and runny. Around the outside, the rock forms a hard crust.

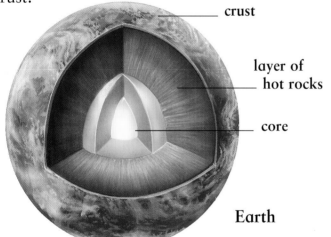

crust

layer of hot rocks

core

Earth

▷ Millions of years ago, the land on Earth was joined together in one huge continent. Gradually, it split up and formed the continents we have today. These are still moving slowly. Millions of years from now, the surface of the Earth will look very different from the way it does now.

▽ The Earth's crust is made up of enormous sections called plates. These move very, very slowly. Sometimes they push against each other and crumple. When this happens, mountains form.

Fact box
• People once thought that the Earth was flat and you could fall off the edge.

Find out more
Air and
Atmosphere
Day and Night
Solar System
Volcano
Water
Weather

Eel

Because they are long and thin, and have wriggly bodies, you may think that eels are a type of snake. In fact, they are fish. Like fish, they are scaly and have thin fins that run the length of their bodies.

▷ The moray eel can grow up to 10 feet long. It hides by day in holes in the rocks, and only comes out at night. It eats shellfish but will attack humans if disturbed.

▽ To breed, freshwater eels have to swim thousands of miles—from lakes and rivers in America and Europe, to the Sargasso Sea, near Bermuda. The eels' eggs hatch there and drift north in an ocean current. Up to three years later the young eels wriggle back into the rivers again.

Fact box

• Young eels are called elvers.
• There are about 600 kinds of eel, living in fresh and salt water all over the world.
• To reach lakes further inland, freshwater eels slither overland across damp grass.

△ The electric eel of South America eats small fish. It catches them by stunning the fish with an electric shock. This shock is so strong that it could knock down a human.

Find out more
Goldfish and Carp
Shellfish

Electric current

Electricity is a type of energy. It can move along wires. When it flows along a wire this is called an electric current. Electricity is used to make heat, light, sound, and movement—it can make all kinds of machines work. Electricity can be stored in batteries too.

△ You can make a kind of electricity. Rub a balloon on a wool sweater. The static electricity will hold the balloon to the wall.

⚠ Never touch an electrical socket. Electricity can kill you.

▷ To light the bulb, electricity flows from the battery down the wire through the bulb and back to the battery. This is called a circuit.

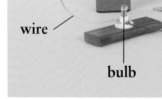

battery

wire

bulb

◁ None of these machines could work without electricity. Someday even cars may be electric.

Find out more
....
Cars
Energy
Light
Trains
Weather

Electricity

Electricity is a form of energy. It is also known as electrical energy. We get some electricity from batteries, but most of the electricity in our homes is made in power plants. It reaches our homes along thick cables. The electricity flows along these, like a current in a stream. This is why we call it current electricity. Electricity that does not flow in a current is called static electricity.

△ A flash of lightning is a huge spark of electricity. Static electricity forms in clouds and jumps through the air. It may travel from cloud to cloud, or down to the ground.

▽ Run a plastic comb through your hair quickly, several times. Hold the comb over some bits of paper and see how it attracts the paper. Combing your hair made static electricity form on the comb. Static electricity on an object can make it attract other objects.

△ Electricity only flows along wires if they are joined in a loop called a circuit. In a flashlight, a circuit joins one end of a battery to the other, through a bulb and a switch. The circuit here works in the same way. The bulb will only light up if there is no gap anywhere in the circuit.

▷ These tall towers hold up thick electrical wires, or cables. These carry electricity from generating stations to towns and cities. When it gets there, it travels along cables buried under the ground.

Fact box
• Tall buildings and church spires often have a metal pole leading from the top to the ground. This is called a lightning rod. If the building is struck by lightning, the rod carries the electricity safely to the ground.

◁ These model cars are controlled by changing the amount of electricity flowing in the metal racetrack. In many machines, the flow of electricity is controlled using electronics, which are very tiny but complicated circuits.

▽ There is an electric motor in this model train. Electricity flows along the metal tracks and into the train. It makes the motor spin, and this moves the wheels of the train. When the electricity stops, the train stops.

Find out more
Battery
Calculator
Computers
Energy
Magnets

Elephant

Elephants are the heaviest land animals. They are also intelligent and have good memories. There are two species: one lives in Africa, another in India. They use their long trunks almost like an arm, to put food and water in their mouths. Their tusks are made of ivory and males use them for fighting.

△ In India, elephants are trained to do heavy work, such as lifting logs. An elephant driver, or keeper, is called a mahout.

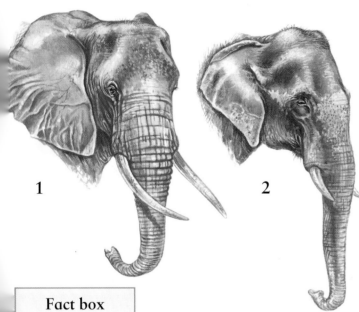

1   2

◁ **1** The African elephant is bigger than its Indian cousin. It has bigger tusks and ears and a hollow forehead. The tusks are really teeth that grow outside the mouth.

◁ **2** The Indian elephant has smaller ears and a rounded forehead. Only the male Indian elephant has tusks.

▽ In Africa, elephants live in small family groups ruled by the oldest females. Males live in all-male herds.

Fact box
• African elephants grow to 13 feet, over twice as tall as an adult human.
• They can weigh over 7 tons—heavier than six cars.
• Elephants can live to be 70.

Find out more
Giraffe
Hippopotamus
Rhinoceros

Elk

There are two kinds of elk. One lives in Canada and the United States; the other lives in northern Europe and looks like the American moose. They are both large members of the deer family.

△ The American elk is known as a wapiti. Wapiti are closely related to the red deer of Europe. Like all deer, wapiti mainly eat fresh shoots and fruit.

▷ European elk are usually born as twins in the spring. They are unsteady on their feet at first, but are soon able to trot at a fast pace.

▷ Wapiti calves are born in the spring. Their white-spotted coats act as camouflage and help them hide from wolves and pumas.

◁ Male European elk, like American moose, grow huge spoon-shaped antlers. They use them to challenge other males and show off to the females. The older the male, the larger his antlers. The mating season in the fall is called the rut. At this time, male elks fill the air with low, grunting noises.

Find out more
Deer
Mammal
Reindeer

Energy

Nothing can happen without energy. Energy is what makes everything work, including you. There are many different types of energy. There is movement energy, light energy, heat energy, chemical energy, and electrical energy. Energy can change from one type to another, but it cannot be made from scratch or destroyed.

△ Sound is a type of energy. Beating the drum makes a sound which travels through the air in waves. When the waves reach your ears, you hear the sound.

△ This is New York. In a big city like this, huge amounts of energy are needed to heat, light, and give power to offices and homes, and to make buses, cars, and trains run.

▽ Plants use energy from sunshine to make food for themselves. All living things, including plants and animals, need energy from food to stay alive. Some animals eat plants, some eat other animals, and some eat both. In the end, all plants and animals get the energy they need from the Sun.

energy from the Sun

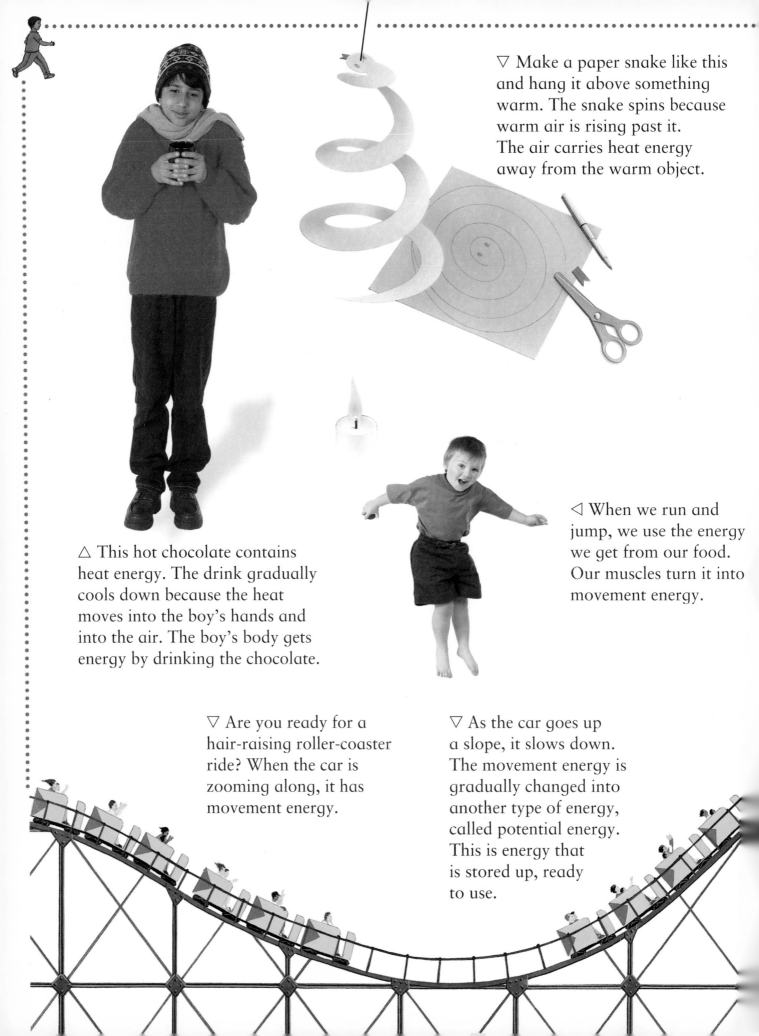

▽ Make a paper snake like this and hang it above something warm. The snake spins because warm air is rising past it. The air carries heat energy away from the warm object.

△ This hot chocolate contains heat energy. The drink gradually cools down because the heat moves into the boy's hands and into the air. The boy's body gets energy by drinking the chocolate.

◁ When we run and jump, we use the energy we get from our food. Our muscles turn it into movement energy.

▽ Are you ready for a hair-raising roller-coaster ride? When the car is zooming along, it has movement energy.

▽ As the car goes up a slope, it slows down. The movement energy is gradually changed into another type of energy, called potential energy. This is energy that is stored up, ready to use.

▽ Along the coast of Norway, in northern Europe, there are deep inlets of sea with steep sides, called fjords.

◁ In Sweden, people dance around a maypole on Midsummer's Eve to mark the longest day of the year.

▷ Olive trees grow in rows on the hot, dry hills of southern Spain. Lots of European countries grow olives and many other fruits.

◁ Budapest is the capital of Hungary. It used to be two cities—Buda and Pest. The Danube River ran between them. Now it flows through the middle of Budapest. There are many fine old buildings along the Danube's banks.

Find out more

History
World

Evolution

Millions of years have passed since life first started on Earth. The animals that lived then are very different from those that are found now. This is because things evolve (change) over time to stand a better chance of survival.

△ **1** Fossils are the remains of animals that died millions of years ago. They are a good way of telling how things have evolved. You can find fossils on some beaches and in certain types of rock formations.

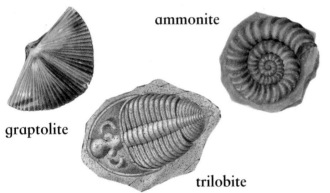

ammonite

graptolite

trilobite

△ **2** Look at fossils with a magnifying glass. You will see that they look fairly similar to some animals still alive today. The way they have changed shows how they have evolved in order to survive.

◁ Once there was just one type of fox, but new forms evolved. The Arctic fox has thick fur to keep warm, and is colored white for camouflage.

▷ The desert fox has evolved to deal with the hot desert. It has large ears to help it keep cool, and is sandy in color.

◁ The peppered moth has evolved very recently. Usually this moth is light-colored but a black-winged form is found in places where the trees have been blackened by smoke from factories. This gives it better camouflage.

Find out more
Birds
Camouflage
Habitat

Experiment

Scientists are always trying to find out more about the world we live in. They try out their ideas using tests, called experiments. Some experiments are very quick and easy to do. Others are very long and complicated. Some do not work well the first time and have to be done again. Here is an experiment you can do: a test to see which ball bounces highest.

△ **1** You will need different kinds of balls, such as a tennis ball and a soft sponge ball, and paper and pencil to record the information. You also need to make a long measuring stick and mark it in feet or meters.

▷ **4** Study your results. What do they show? Before you did the experiment, did you guess how high each ball would bounce? Were you right?

◁ **2** Get a friend to hold the measure straight. Now drop each ball from the same height. Before you drop a ball, try guessing how high it will bounce.

△ **3** Note the type of ball and how high it bounces. Write this down and compare the results.

Find out more

Biology

Chemistry and Chemicals

Energy

Physics

Farming

All over the world, farmers grow crops and raise animals for food. They plant fields of wheat, rice, corn, oats, and vegetables. They raise animals for their meat, milk, and eggs. On smaller farms a lot of the work is done by hand. Large farms need machines for much of the work.

bread

pasta

▽ Rice is an important crop in China, India, and other countries in Asia. It is grown in flooded fields called paddies. It is usually sown and picked by hand.

▷ Wheat is almost always grown in huge fields. It is harvested by a combine harvester. Wheat grain is ground up into flour to make bread and pasta.

rice

△ Milk from cows is used to make dairy products such as cheese, butter, and cream.

△ Female chickens are called hens. They lay eggs. People eat meat and eggs from chickens.

◁ Large flocks of sheep are raised on sheep stations in Australia. Their wool is clipped off, cleaned, and spun into yarn.

◁ Pests, such as the Colorado potato beetle, destroy crops. Farmers spray the crops with chemicals to kill the pests.

△ This tractor is spreading manure over a plowed field. Manure is a fertilizer. It feeds the soil and helps new crops to grow large and strong.

Find out more

Asia

Australia and the Pacific islands

Conservation

Europe

Colorado potato beetle

Fish

Fish live in water. Some live in the cold ocean, others live in warm, shallow water. Fish are all different shapes and sizes. The huge but toothless whale shark can be up to 14 yards (15 meters) long. A tiny fish called a pygmy goby is no longer than your fingernail.

eye

fin

gill cover

fin

scale

tail

great white shark

◁ Great white sharks are fast swimmers and fierce hunters. They use their razor-sharp teeth to tear apart their prey.

▽ Blue marlin and many other big fish live far away from the shore. Tuna and mackerel live close to the surface of the ocean. Sawfish and rays live on the ocean floor.

blue marlin

tuna

mackerel

ray

sawfish

puffer fish

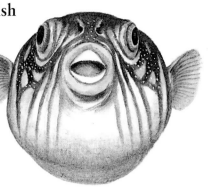

African cichlid

▷ A puffer fish can blow up its body like a balloon. It does this to scare away its enemies.

▷ The babies of the African cichlid fish swim into their mother's mouth to escape from danger.

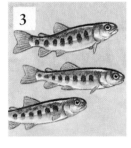
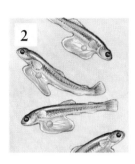

△ **1** A female salmon lays her eggs in the river where she was born. **2** When the eggs hatch, the babies are called fry.

△ **3** The young salmon live in the river for two years. **4** Then they swim down to the sea. They return to the river to lay their eggs.

Fact box
• A fish is a vertebrate, which means that it has a backbone.
• Fish breathe by taking in oxygen from the water through their gills.
• Most fish swim through the water by moving their tails from side to side.

lion fish

▽ Fish that live in the warm, shallow water around coral reefs are often brightly colored. Their bold patterns act as camouflage and help them to hide among the corals and to creep up on their prey.

angelfish

parrot fish

butterfly fish

Find out more
Animals
Food
Oceans and seas
Prehistoric life
Water

cowfish

Flamingo, Heron, and Stork

Flamingos live in colonies on shallow lakes in Africa, South America, and Asia. They are pink with large wings, slim necks, and long, thin legs for wading in water. The largest is the great flamingo, which is 5 feet tall. Flamingos, herons, and storks are all in the same group of birds.

▽ Herons are long-legged like flamingos. They wade along the edges of lakes and rivers, hunting for fish. When they spot one, they spear it with their sharp beak. Like most wading birds, they often stand on one leg. This keeps the leg out of the water warm.

▽ Storks are also wading birds. White storks spend the winter in Africa, and in the summer fly to Europe to breed. Many Europeans think storks bring good luck. They build platforms on their chimneys so the birds can make their nests on them.

△ Flamingos wade through the shallows moving their heads from side to side. Their specially shaped beaks act like strainers, filtering shrimp and other tiny animals from the muddy water. Flamingos get their pink color from the shrimp they eat.

Find out more
Duck and Goose
Pelican
Swan

Flight

Things that fly need an upward push, or force, to keep them in the air. This force is called lift. Without lift, another force, called gravity, pulls them back toward the ground. Aircraft, birds, and insects all have wings. As they fly along, their wings use the air to make lift.

▷ Birds have strong muscles which make their wings flap up and down. Some birds, such as this seabird, have long, thin wings. They use them to glide as well as flap.

△ These balloons are full of hot air. Hot air is lighter than cold air, so the balloons are lighter than the air around them. This means they can float up into the air.

△ Some small aircraft have a propeller at the front. This is like a fan. It spins very fast, pushing air backwards and pulling the aircraft through the air.

◁ An aircraft's wings only make lift when the aircraft is speeding through the air. The air flows over and under the wing. Because of the wing's special curved shape, this makes lift.

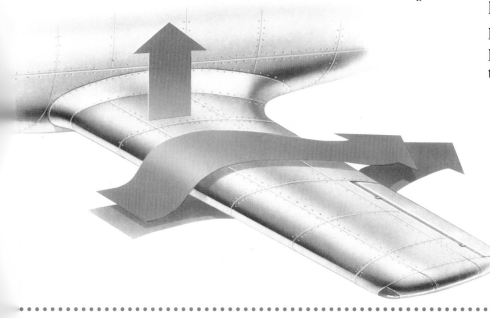

115

◁ Some seeds, such as these dandelion seeds, are very light and fluffy. They drift with the breeze until they reach a good place for growing.

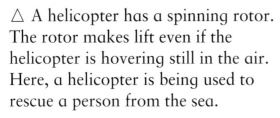

△ A helicopter has a spinning rotor. The rotor makes lift even if the helicopter is hovering still in the air. Here, a helicopter is being used to rescue a person from the sea.

◁ Blow hard on a dandelion. Watch the seeds. How long is it before they reach the ground?

◁ Put a piece of tissue paper on your bottom lip and blow gently to make air flow across the top of the paper. The tissue paper lifts up. A wing works in the same way. Its shape makes air flow faster over the top than the bottom.

Find out more

Air and Atmosphere

Engines

Floating

Force

Space exploration

Floating

Why do some things float in water, and some things sink? Think about the space something takes up. This space is called its volume.

Things float if they weigh less than the same volume of water. A beach ball floats in water because it does not weigh as much as water with the same volume. A coin weighs more than water with the same volume, so it sinks.

△ These logs are floating down the river from the forest to the lumber mill. They float well because wood is lighter than water.

▷ Test a few objects to see if they float. Then choose something that floats and try pushing it down into the water. Can you feel the water pushing it upward? This upward push is called upthrust. Upthrust is the force that makes things float.

Fact box

• It's easier to float in salty water than in freshwater. The Dead Sea, between Israel and Jordan, is so salty that you can float without having to swim.

◁ A submarine can float or sink. To make it sink, water is let into tanks in the submarine's hull. This makes it heavier. To make it float again, air is pumped into the tanks to empty the water out. This makes it lighter.

Find out more
Flight
Force
Water

Flowers

Most plants have flowers. They are important because they help to make the seeds that grow into new plants. This happens when a grain called pollen goes from one flower to another. Large, sticky pollen grains are carried by insects, when they fly from flower to flower drinking nectar. Small, light grains are carried by the wind.

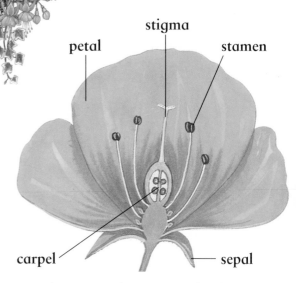

hanging basket

stigma
petal
stamen
carpel
sepal

△ These are the parts of a flower. Pollen is carried from the stamen of one flower to the stigma of another. This is called pollination.

▷ Flowers make nectar, from which bees makes honey. As the bee drinks the nectar, pollen sticks to its body. When it flies to another flower, some pollen rubs off onto that flower and pollinates it.

pollen

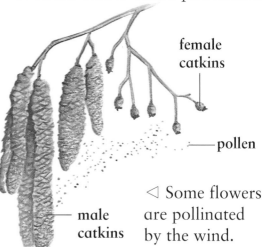

female catkins

pollen

male catkins

◁ Some flowers are pollinated by the wind. Pollen is blown from the male catkins to the female catkins.

 1

 2

 3

 4

Find out more
Conservation
Insects
Plants
Seasons
Water

△ **1** The flowers of a pear tree are pollinated by insects. **2** Tiny fruits grow under the flowers. Inside each fruit are seeds.

△ **3** The fruits swell and grow. **4** When the fruits are ripe, animals break the fruits open and the seeds are spread out.

Fly

There are many types of flies, and they are found everywhere. Unlike other insects, they have just one pair of wings for flying; their tiny back wings are only used for balance. A few flies carry deadly diseases, but many help plants by carrying pollen from one flower to another.

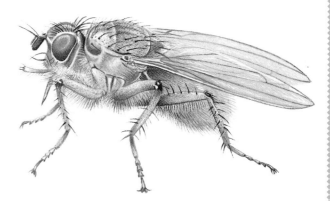

△ The African tsetse fly carries a disease called sleeping sickness. It spreads the disease from wild animals to humans and livestock by biting them and drinking their blood.

Fact box

• House flies beat their wings 200 times a second.
• Gnats beat their wings 1,000 times a second. This is what makes the buzzing sound common to all flies.

△ The hover fly, also called the flower fly, gets its name from the fact that it hovers around flowers. Hover flies have markings like wasps.

▽ Like all flies, dung flies spend the first part of their lives as maggots. During this time, they live inside the dung left by animals. They feed on the dung and, in doing so, clear it up.

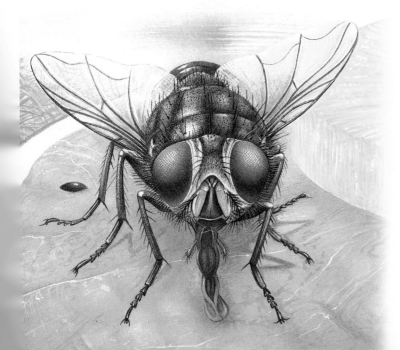

◁ Bluebottles (left) and house flies feed on all kinds of food. They have "taste buds" on their feet. These tell them whether something they have landed on is good to eat.

Find out more
Ant and Termite
Bee and Wasp
Beetle
Insect

Flying machines

There are all kinds of different flying machines, from hot-air balloons and gliders, to helicopters and passenger planes. The fastest way to travel is by airplane. An airplane has wings to lift it up into the air and an engine to push it forward. For hundreds of years people dreamed of being able to fly, but they were not successful until the early 1900s.

△ The first airplane was built by the Wright brothers in the early 1900s. The pilot had to lie on his stomach to fly it.

▷ This passenger jet can carry about 250 people. Jumbo jets are the largest passenger planes in the world. They can carry more than 400 people.

▽ This is a fighter plane. It is called a jump jet because it can take off straight up into the air. It can also hover above the ground.

jump jet

hot air balloon

△ The air inside a hot-air balloon is heated by a powerful gas burner. Because hot air rises, it makes the balloon float up into the sky.

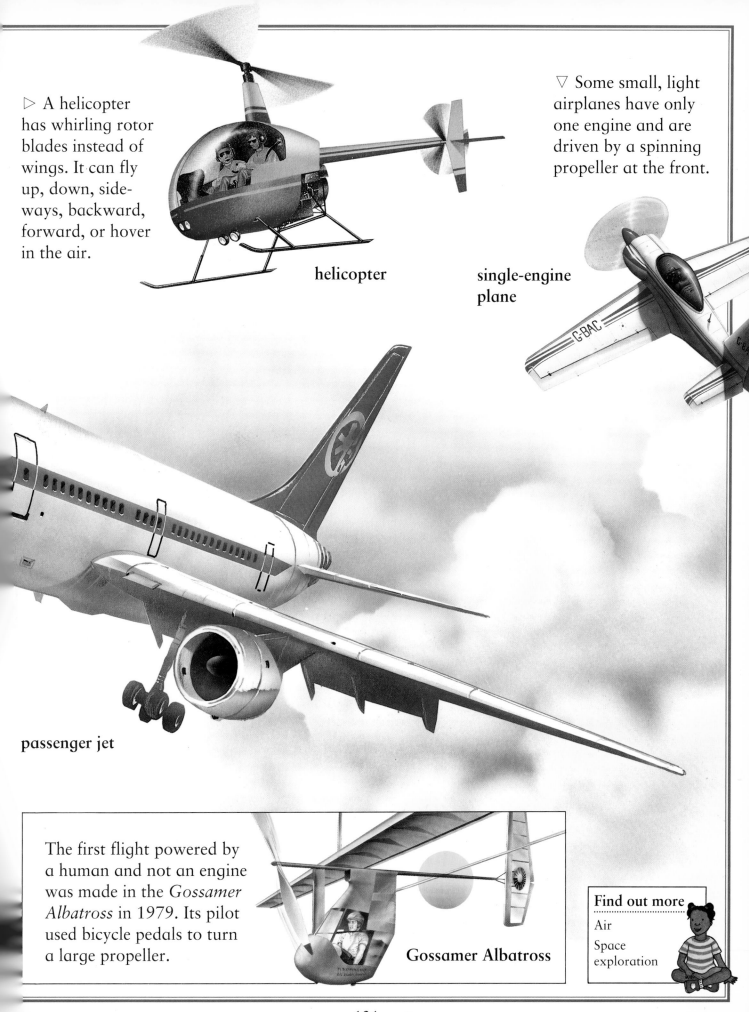

▷ A helicopter has whirling rotor blades instead of wings. It can fly up, down, sideways, backward, forward, or hover in the air.

helicopter

▽ Some small, light airplanes have only one engine and are driven by a spinning propeller at the front.

single-engine plane

passenger jet

The first flight powered by a human and not an engine was made in the *Gossamer Albatross* in 1979. Its pilot used bicycle pedals to turn a large propeller.

Gossamer Albatross

Find out more

Air

Space exploration

Food

Everybody needs food. It gives you energy to move and to keep warm. It helps you to grow, and to get better when you are sick. To stay healthy you need proteins, fats, carbohydrates, fiber, and vitamins, as well as water to drink. Eating too much sugary or fatty food is unhealthy.

proteins

△ Milk, meat, eggs, nuts, and fish give you proteins that build your body and help it to stay strong.

▷ Fruit and vegetables have fiber. Fiber helps the food you eat to pass through your body.

fiber

fats

△ Fats from foods, like butter, milk, cheese, bacon, and oil give you energy, but it is best not to eat large amounts of fat.

carbohydrates

△ Carbohydrates give your body lots of energy. Foods like bread, pasta, potatoes, beans, and rice all have carbohydrates in them.

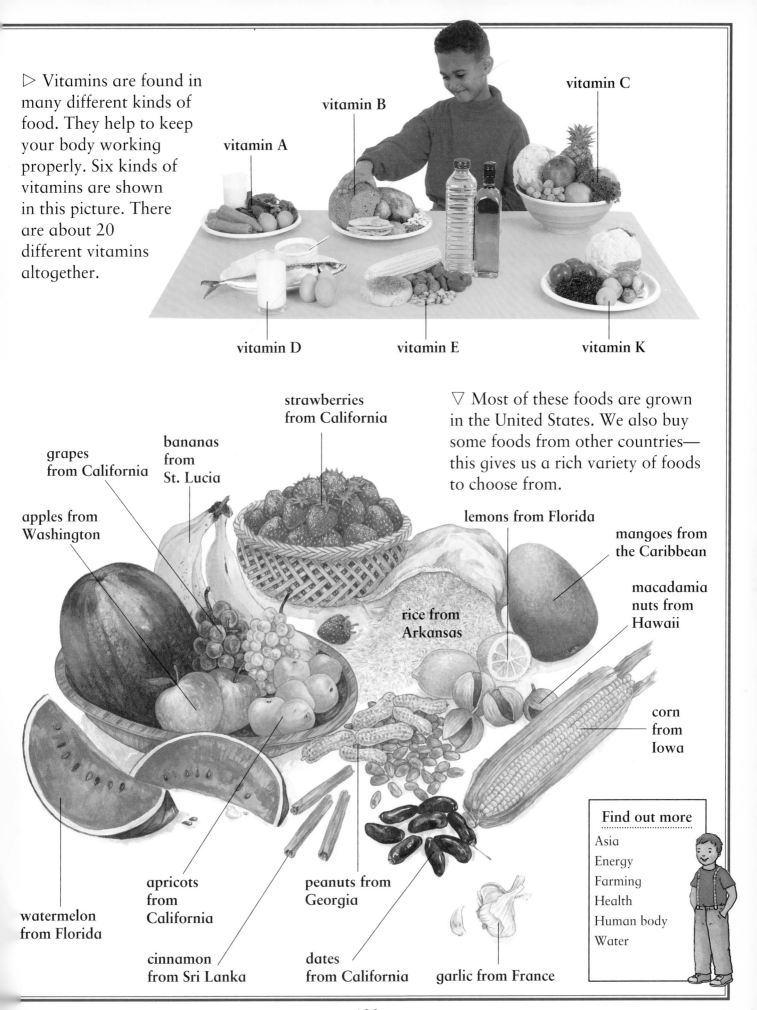

▷ Vitamins are found in many different kinds of food. They help to keep your body working properly. Six kinds of vitamins are shown in this picture. There are about 20 different vitamins altogether.

vitamin A

vitamin B

vitamin C

vitamin D

vitamin E

vitamin K

strawberries from California

▽ Most of these foods are grown in the United States. We also buy some foods from other countries—this gives us a rich variety of foods to choose from.

grapes from California

bananas from St. Lucia

apples from Washington

lemons from Florida

mangoes from the Caribbean

macadamia nuts from Hawaii

rice from Arkansas

corn from Iowa

apricots from California

peanuts from Georgia

watermelon from Florida

cinnamon from Sri Lanka

dates from California

garlic from France

Find out more

Asia
Energy
Farming
Health
Human body
Water

Force

A force is a push or a pull. Forces can make things move. For example, to throw a ball, you push it hard to make it move quickly through the air. You also need a force to stop something moving. When you catch a ball, your hands push against it to slow it down. Engines and motors make forces that cause machines to move. The force of gravity pulls everything downward toward the Earth.

△ This boy is pulling on the bar. He exerts a force that lifts him up. When he lets go, the force of gravity pulls him down to the ground.

▽ The force of gravity pulls this girl down the slide. Another force, called friction, slows her down slightly. But because the surface of the slide is smooth, she hardly notices. There is more friction if surfaces are rough.

◁ Forces can squash or stretch things. When this boy jumps on his pogo stick he squashes the ball under his feet. The ball then pushes him back upward into the air.

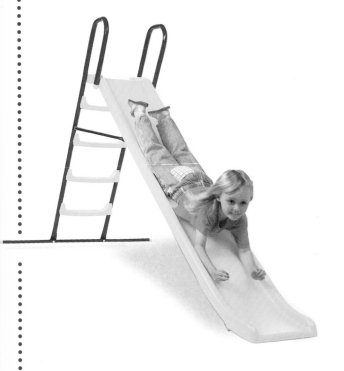

▷ These children are both exerting the same amount of force on the rope, but the forces are pulling in opposite directions. The two forces cancel each other out, so the rope does not move and neither do the children.

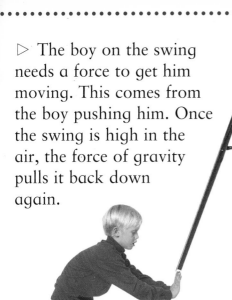

▷ The boy on the swing needs a force to get him moving. This comes from the boy pushing him. Once the swing is high in the air, the force of gravity pulls it back down again.

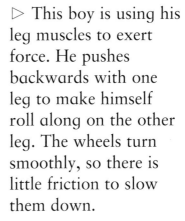

▷ This boy is using his leg muscles to exert force. He pushes backwards with one leg to make himself roll along on the other leg. The wheels turn smoothly, so there is little friction to slow them down.

▷ In these pictures, arrows show the direction the force is pushing or pulling. This girl is pushing as hard as she can.

△ It's much easier when two people push. The more force that is exerted on the sled, the more quickly it will speed up.

Forests

The forests that grow in cold, dry parts of the Earth have very different kinds of trees from the forests that grow in warm, wet parts of the world.

A forest is home to many animals. The trees give them food, and shelter them from the Sun, rain, and wind.

△ Look at all these things. Wood from trees has been used to make them. Even the pages of this book are made from wood.

◁ Rain forests grow in hot, wet places. More than half of the world's animals and plants live in these forests. Huge areas of rain forest are cut down each year. This means that many of the animals and plants could die out.

deciduous forests

◁ Deciduous forests are full of trees that lose their leaves in the fall. New leaves grow in the spring.

badger

white-tailed deer

jay

△ The badger lives in an underground home called a set. It hunts in the forest at night.

△ Deer's spots make them hard to see in the forest. This is called camouflage.

◁ Jays eat the acorns from oak trees. They often bury the acorns, then dig them up in the winter when it is hard to find food.

coniferous forests

▷ Forests in cold places are full of coniferous trees. They keep their leaves all through the year.

moose

chipmunk

◁ A moose is a very large deer. It feeds on water plants and young tree shoots.

△ A chipmunk uses pouches in its cheeks to carry nuts and seeds back to store in its burrow.

Find out more
Buildings
Conservation
Mountains
Trees
Trucks

Fossils

Fossils are what is left of plants and animals long after they die. Scientists study fossils to find out about life on Earth millions of years ago. When the plants and animals died, what was left of them very slowly turned to stone.

▷ Nearly 200 years ago, 12-year-old Mary Anning found a huge fossil in a cliff. It was a reptile called Plesiosaurus that lived in the sea millions of years ago.

spider in amber

△ 1 Ammonites lived in the sea millions of years ago. 2 When one died, its soft body rotted away. Layers of mud buried its hard shell.

△ 3 Over thousands of years, the mud hardened and turned to rock, and the shell became a fossil. 4 Many years later the fossil was dug up.

▷ This woolly mammoth was frozen for thousands of years in the icy ground of Siberia, in Russia.

woolly mammoth

△ This spider has been kept whole in amber. Amber is sticky tree sap which has dried and hardened.

◁ Fossils of plants are often found in large lumps of coal. This is a type of fern.

Find out more
Dinosaurs
Prehistoric life

Fox

Foxes are small wild dogs with short legs and big, bushy tails. They are skillful hunters that come out at night and rest by day in burrows called dens. The female is called a vixen, the male is a dog, and the young are cubs.

good hearing —————

sharp eyesight —————

excellent sense ————— of smell

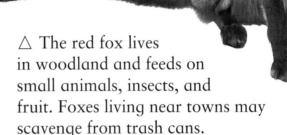

△ The red fox lives in woodland and feeds on small animals, insects, and fruit. Foxes living near towns may scavenge from trash cans.

◁ Foxes are found in most parts of the world. The fennec fox lives in the deserts of North Africa and Arabia. During the day it stays below ground in its burrow to avoid the heat of the sun. Its huge ears also help it lose heat and keep cool.

▷ Foxes' pointed ears give them very good hearing. This helps them detect the slightest noise of a small animal in the grass. Roll two pieces of cardboard into cones and hold them to your ears. Get a friend to make a noise behind you, then hear for yourself the difference with the cones and without.

Find out more
Dog (domestic)
Dog (wild)

Friction

Friction is a force which tries to stop one surface sliding against another. There is more friction between rough surfaces than between smooth surfaces. Friction stops your feet sliding on the ground as you walk. It stops things slipping from your grasp, and stops bicycle tires skidding when you brake. Look out for friction at home or at school.

△ Find out how different surfaces are affected by friction. Slide different objects down a slope. Try coins, pens and pencils, and an eraser. Which ones slide most easily?

Fact box
• When surfaces rub together, friction makes heat. That's why you rub your hands to warm them up.

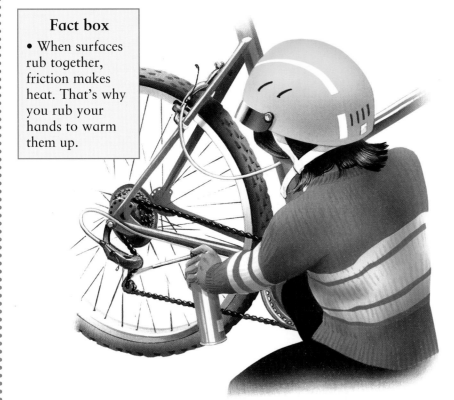

◁ This girl is putting oil on her bicycle gears and chain. The oil reduces friction. It lets the gear wheels turn more easily and makes the chain more flexible. This makes pedaling easier and stops the gears from wearing out. Oil also stops the metal parts from rusting.

◁ Friction also tries to slow things down that are moving through the air. There is less air friction on things with a smooth, streamlined shape, such as this sports car.

Find out more
Air and Atmosphere
Force
Machines
Water

Goat

Hardy and good at climbing, goats can survive in the highest mountains. Wild goats are found across the Northern Hemisphere. Tame goats are kept for their milk, meat, and skin.

feral goat

Cretan wild goat

Apennine mountain goat

△ Kashmir and Angora goats are valued for their fine wool. The long, silky coat of the Angora (above) gives mohair or angora wool. Kashmir goats give cashmere wool.

▽ Ibexes are wild goats found in Europe, Africa, and Asia. They live on the mountaintops in the summer, and move to warmer lower pastures in the winter.

Fact box
• Goats' hooves have hard edges and soft centers. They act like suction cups on slippery rocks.
• Goats give off a very strong smell.
• A young goat is a called a kid, a female is a doe or a nanny, and a male is a billy.

△ Goats were first tamed 10,000 years ago, and there are now many breeds. They like to eat grass and plants, but they will eat almost anything and can survive on thorn trees and shrubs. Male goats are often bad-tempered and use their long, curved horns to fight each other for females.

Find out more
Antelope
Cow and Bull
Yak

Goldfish and Carp

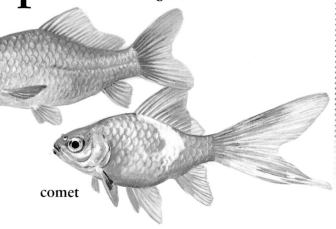

common goldfish

comet

Goldfish and carp originally came from lakes and streams in Asia and were first introduced into the United States in the late 1800s. Goldfish are often small and brightly colored; carp are larger and usually have plainer coloring.

△ Goldfish survive well in both outdoor ponds and indoor tanks. They come in a wide range of colors and shapes.

△ **1** Taking care of goldfish is easy. You will need a tank with clean gravel and a few large objects. You should also put in some water plants to give the fish oxygen to breathe.

▷ **2** Fill the tank with water and carefully place the goldfish in the tank. You will need to feed them daily, and you must be sure to clean the tank and change the water regularly.

silver carp

△ Carp are found in North America, Asia, and Europe. Grass carp are helpful to humans because they eat pondweed. In China, the silver carp is bred for food.

Find out more
Eel
Fish
Salmon and Trout

Gorilla

Gorillas are huge and powerful apes. They look fierce, but are actually gentle vegetarians. They are now very rare and are found only in the forests and mountains of Central Africa.

▽ Gorillas live in family groups. These are led by a big male called a silverback, who gets his name from the silver hairs on his back. These hairs grow when a male gorilla is about ten years old. Silverbacks may be as tall as a man and weigh 500 pounds—about three times as much as a man.

△ Gorillas eat leaves and buds, stalks, berries, and sometimes even tree bark. When they have eaten most of the food in one place, they move on to let the plants grow back again.

◁▽ Gorillas learn to walk at about ten months. They feed on their mother's milk for the first two years and spend much of their time playing. They sleep with their mothers until they are three years old, then they make their own nests of leaves and branches.

Find out more
Baboon
Chimpanzee
Monkey
Orangutan

Grasslands

Grasslands cover huge areas of the world. These lands are sometimes too dry for many trees to grow there. Grasses are tough plants that grow quickly.

The hot grassland of Africa is called savanna, and in Australia it is called the bush. Grasslands are called pampas in South America, prairies in North America, and steppes in Asia.

▽ The African savanna often looks brown and dry. In the short rainy season it is fresh and green.

△ In Australia the bush may catch fire in the dry season. The ashes that are left become part of the soil.

△ Huge areas of the prairies of North America are used to grow wheat.

◁ This type of grass grows on the pampas of South America. It has long, feathery flowers.

pampas grass

Find out more
Africa
Asia
Camouflage
Farming
North America
South America

138

Guinea pig, Gerbil, and Hamster

Guinea pigs, gerbils, and hamsters are all mammals. These rodents live wild in many parts of the world, but they also make very good pets. They need a good-sized cage and should be given food and water every day. They also enjoy lots of care and attention.

Fact box

• Hamsters are originally from Europe and Asia; guinea pigs, from South America; and gerbils, from Africa and Asia.
• Guinea pigs were taken to Europe as long ago as the 1500s.
• Despite their name, guinea pigs are not related to pigs.

▽ In South America, humans have been eating guinea pig meat for about 4,000 years. Wild guinea pigs, called cavies, still live on the grasslands there.

△ Guinea pigs feed on grass and green plants in the wild, so if you give them dry pet food, make sure they have plenty of water.

▽ Hamsters live alone and come out at night to eat grasses, seeds, and berries. They have big pouches in their cheeks that they use to carry food back to their nests.

▷ Gerbils live on the edges of hot deserts. They hide in burrows by day and come out at night to feed on seeds and insects. Their long back legs and tails help them leap across the hot, sandy ground.

Find out more
Beaver
Mouse
Rabbit and Hare
Rat
Squirrel

Gull

Gulls, or seagulls, are large, sturdy seabirds with webbed feet. There are over 40 species, found in coastal areas all over the world. Sometimes gulls are found inland, in the countryside, and in towns and cities.

△ Gulls eat many different foods, including fish, eggs, earthworms, and insects. They also scavenge for food in garbage dumps.

▽ Baby gulls are covered in soft, fluffy feathers, called down. They are fed by their parents until the chicks have grown their flight feathers.

▽ Gulls are strong fliers, soaring and gliding on the strong sea breezes. Many gulls nest on cliffs, forming large and noisy colonies.

▽ Parents often have to fend off other gulls, like the lesser black-backed gull, that try to eat eggs and chicks from their nests.

Find out more

Albatross
Birds
Duck and Goose
Seabird

Habitat

A habitat is the place where an animal lives. It provides the animal with food, water, and shelter—everything it needs to survive. There are many different habitats all over the world.

◁ Minibeasts like slugs and snails prefer a habitat that is dark and damp. Leave a flowerpot upside-down in your yard with one edge propped up. Go back to it a few days later, and you may find it has become a habitat to some minibeasts.

savanna

rain forest

desert

△ Over time, animals have evolved to survive in their own habitats. For example, the camel is able to live in the desert because it can go for days without drinking. If a habitat changes—for example, if the rainfall decreases—each animal must adapt to the new environment. Unlike humans, if an animal is suddenly taken out of its habitat it cannot adapt quickly enough and is unlikely to survive.

Find out more

Camel
Chimpanzee
Evolution
Giraffe

Health

You need to be healthy to keep your body working properly. A healthy diet gives your body energy and helps it to grow and repair itself. Exercise helps your body to grow and stay strong. Caring for yourself will keep you fit and healthy. Keeping clean helps to kill the germs that can cause sickness.

◁ Exercise makes your muscles strong and keeps your body fit. Playing soccer and other active games is a good way to exercise.

△ To get all the things you need for a strong, healthy body and energy you have to eat many different foods. You also have to drink lots of water.

▽ Washing with soap and water keeps your skin clean. Keeping clean stops germs from spreading.

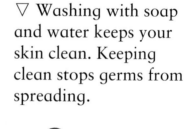

Fact box

• The outside of your teeth is protected with hard enamel. Sugary food and drink eats the enamel away.

• People are given injections, called vaccinations, to keep them from getting sick.

• Most children sleep for about 10 hours every night.

▷ If you scrape your skin, you should clean it so that germs cannot get in. Germs are tiny living things. Some of them can make you sick.

▽ Your body needs sleep to give your brain and muscles time to rest. When you are asleep, your body also has time to grow.

▷ Dentists look after teeth. If they find a hole, they may fill it. Don't have too much candy and soda, and brush your teeth every day to keep them clean.

◁ Doctors look after you when you are sick. They may listen to your heart or look down your throat. They will give you medicine if you need any to help you get better.

Find out more
Food
Human body
Sports
Water

143

Hedgehog

Hedgehogs are mammals found in the woods and hedges of Europe, Asia, and Africa. Most have thousands of thick spines covering their backs, which help protect them from predators. There are also hairy hedgehogs, which live in Asia.

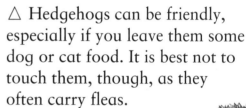

△ Hedgehogs can be friendly, especially if you leave them some dog or cat food. It is best not to touch them, though, as they often carry fleas.

▽ The common hedgehog usually has about four babies. The babies do not get stung when they drink their mother's milk, because she only has spines on her back. Adults go out after dark to hunt for food. They will eat plants, but prefer insects and frogs.

Fact box

• Babies are born blind, with soft spines.
• Hedgehogs spend more than 20 hours a day sleeping. In cold northern regions, they hibernate in the winter, curling up under a pile of leaves.
• One hedgehog, the moon rat of Sumatra, can be 16 inches long.

△ When a hedgehog senses danger, it curls up into a tight ball with its spines on the outside. This discourages most predators, although many hedgehogs are killed by cars when they curl up on roads. They are able to climb trees, and if they fall, the spines act as a cushion.

Find out more

Fox

Mole

Hippopotamus

These huge animals have large barrel-shaped bodies and short legs. The name hippopotamus comes from Greek and means "river horse." Although they are not related to horses, they do live near rivers—in Africa.

▷ Hippos spend the day in the water with just their eyes, nose, and ears showing. This stops them from getting sunburned. They can stay underwater for up to ten minutes before having to come up for air.

Fact box

• Hippos live in groups of up to 15 in rivers, lakes, and ponds across Africa.
• They can grow to 15 feet long, stand 5 feet at the shoulder, and weigh as much as 5 tons.
• Hippos are related to pigs.

△ Hippos have gigantic mouths with two huge tusks on the bottom jaw. In the breeding season, competing males show off the size of their mouths and may cut each other with their tusks. Hippos leave the water at night and travel to look for the grasses they eat. They have hard lips, which they use to cut the grass.

◁ Baby hippos can weigh 120 pounds at birth. They can stand within minutes of being born, and must stay close to their mother for protection.

Find out more
Horse
Pig
Rhinoceros

145

History

History is the study of what happened in the past. Historians discover facts about the past by reading old books and documents. They find clues in paintings, old buildings, maps, and photographs. Archaeologists study the past by looking for things people made and used. They search for ruined buildings and buried objects, such as tools, weapons, and pots, which tell them how people lived long ago.

△ Older people can tell you about events and daily life when they were young. Their childhood was probably very different from yours.

◁ Archaeologists can find clues about the past in tombs, houses, and bones by digging underground.

▷ Reading books on history is a good way to find out about the past. Television and radio have history programs too.

△ Museums display objects from all over the world. Seeing these objects can help all of us to learn about how people lived in the past.

Ancient Egypt

Some Egyptian pharaohs were buried in pyramids. Their bodies were rowed down the Nile River and sealed inside these large buildings.

△ Studying sites like the pyramids tells us that the Egyptians could carve hard stone, and that they treated their dead rulers with great respect.

Ancient Greece

The Greeks performed plays in open-air theaters. They had a circular floor called an orchestra for dancing, with a stage behind. All the parts were played by male actors who wore masks.

△ There are ruins of many Greek theaters, which tell us how the theater would have looked.

Ancient China

The Great Wall of China is the longest wall ever built. It was built to keep out enemy tribes. The wall had towers for guards to keep watch.

▷ Some of the Great Wall of China still stands today. People can walk along its top.

Ancient Americas

The Aztecs ruled a mighty empire in what is now Mexico. They were fierce warriors. They built pyramids with temples on top, where they made offerings to their gods.

△ Aztec men fastened their cloaks with brooches. This is one made of gold and turquoise.

World War II
Many cities, like Cologne in Germany, were bombed during World War II. The war lasted from 1939 to 1945, and many millions of people died in it.

▷ After the war, new buildings were built in Cologne to replace those that had been destroyed. This shows how the city looks today.

◁ No one knows who carved these enormous stone heads on Easter Island in the Pacific Ocean. We are still learning about the past, but some things may always be a mystery.

Find out more
Art and artists
Books
Castles

Horse

Long legs, a big heart, and large lungs make horses strong and fast—which is why people have used them to ride and to pull carts for 5,000 years. Horses are descended from wild horses that once lived on grassy plains in herds.

dun

dark bay

roan

light bay

palomino

piebald

chestnut

skewbald

gray

black

▷ Horses come in many colors, each with a special name.

◁ Ponies can be kept as family pets. They need a field to live in, and lots of care and attention. They should be exercised regularly and need their hooves trimmed every few weeks.

▽ Grooming keeps a pony's coat glossy and healthy. Be sure never to walk behind a horse or pony—it may kick out in surprise.

▽ Every part, or point, of a horse has a name. Horses are measured in hands. One hand is 4 inches—the average width of a man's hand.

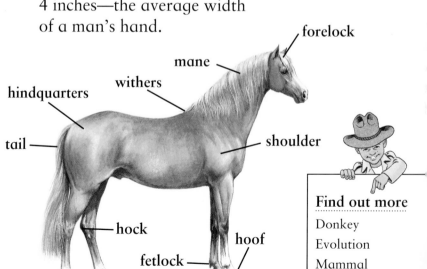

forelock

mane

withers

hindquarters

tail

shoulder

hock

hoof

fetlock

Find out more
Donkey
Evolution
Mammal
Zebra

Human body

Your body is like a complicated machine. Inside and out, it is made up of lots of different working parts. How many do you know? Each of these parts has a job to do. For example, you think with your brain, you chew with your teeth, and you see with your eyes. All these parts work together to keep you alive.

▽ Inside your body, there is a framework of bones, called your skeleton. This supports your body and protects the parts inside it.

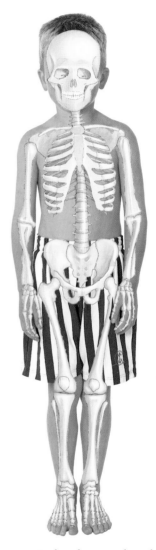

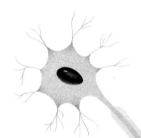

nerve cell

▷ There are millions of tiny cells in your body. They make up every part of you. This is what a muscle cell looks like when you see it through a microscope.

muscle cell

△ Nerve cells are also called neurons. They carry messages between your brain and your body. Some nerve cells are very long. The nerve cells that run down your leg to your toes can be over three feet long.

skin cell

△ Different cells have different shapes and sizes. This is what one of your skin cells looks like.

▽ Everyone's body works the same way, but no one else looks just like you!

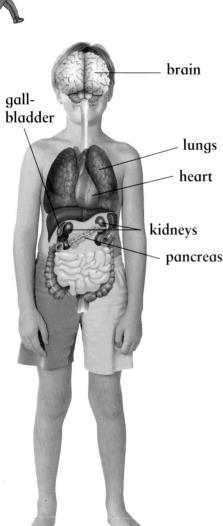

brain

gall-
bladder

lungs

heart

kidneys

pancreas

▷ Some organs link up to form systems. Food travels through your body along your digestive system. Here it is broken into tiny bits and mixed with chemicals. Useful parts of the food pass into your blood and are carried all around your body. Your cells need energy from food to work.

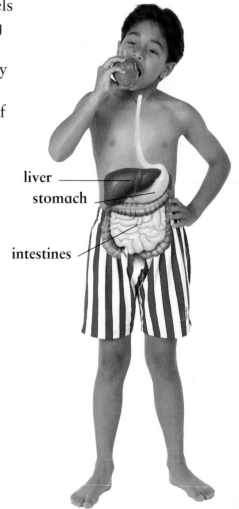

liver
stomach

intestines

◁ Some parts of your body are called organs. Each one has a job to do. Your heart pumps blood around your body. Your lungs help you breathe, and your stomach helps you to digest your food. Your brain lets you think and controls the rest of your body.

▷ Like everything else inside you, blood is made up of cells. There are two kinds of blood cells—red and white. The red cells get their color from a chemical inside them. It carries oxygen from the air you breathe in. All your cells need oxygen to stay alive. White cells help you fight disease. Blood travels around your body along tiny tubes called blood vessels.

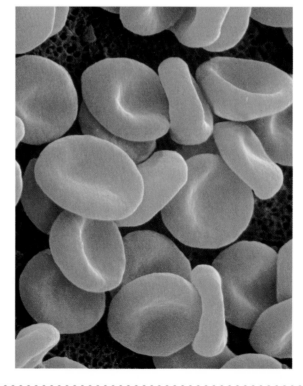

▷ Your heart pumps blood to parts of your body along arteries (colored blue). The blood goes back to your heart along veins (colored red). Then it is pumped to your lungs, and then back around your body again.

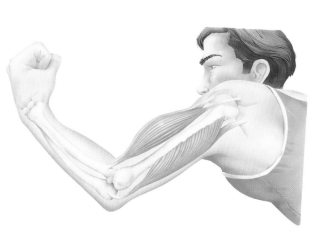

△ When you move, your muscles and bones work together. The muscles in your arm pull on the bones to make your arm bend and straighten.

◁ When you breathe, you draw air down your windpipe into your lungs. Oxygen from the air goes from your lungs into your blood and is carried to all the cells in your body. They need oxygen to stay alive.

◁ Your heart pumps blood around your body. It pumps, or beats, about once every second. Press gently on a friend's wrist. Can you feel it throb as blood surges through the blood vessel there?

Find out more
Biology
Energy
Light and Lenses
Living things
Medicine
Reproduction
Senses

Hummingbird

When hummingbirds hover, their wings beat so fast that they hum, and this gives them their name. These tiny birds live in warm places in North and South America.

▽ Hummingbirds use their long beaks to reach the nectar deep inside flowers.

◁ Hummingbirds use up so much energy beating their wings that they need to feed often. The nectar they eat is full of sugar, which gives them energy quickly.

△ A hummingbird's wings swivel. This means it can hover at a flower while keeping its head perfectly still. It can also fly backward.

Fact box

• Ruby-throated hummingbirds fly 500 miles nonstop across the Gulf of Mexico when migrating.
• Hummingbirds normally lay two eggs, which are the smallest of any bird's.
• There are over 300 species of hummingbird.

▷ All hummingbirds are tiny, but the bee hummingbird of Cuba is the world's smallest bird. It is just 2 inches long— no bigger than a child's thumb.

Find out more
Bird
Migration
Ostrich

Hyena

Hyenas are mammals that live in Africa and Asia. They mainly eat the bones and flesh left by lions after a kill. Their jaws are so strong that they can crush and eat bones that even lions cannot handle.

striped hyena

brown hyena

△ Brown and striped hyenas are smaller and less fierce than spotted hyenas. They often prowl around at night, eating the remains of other animals' kills.

▷ Spotted hyenas are also known as laughing hyenas because of the weird cries they make. The largest and strongest of hyenas, they grow up to 6.5 feet long. Spotted hyenas hunt in packs and will sometimes attack rhinos.

◁ The aardwolf is a close relative of the hyena that lives in southern Africa. It is smaller than a hyena and eats only termites, ants, and insects.

Find out more
Dog (wild)
Fox
Lion

Insects

Insects are animals with six legs. Most insects are tiny and have wings. Even the largest insect, the goliath beetle, is only 4 inches (10 cm) long. Many insects are brightly colored, and some look like leaves or twigs to help them hide from their enemies.

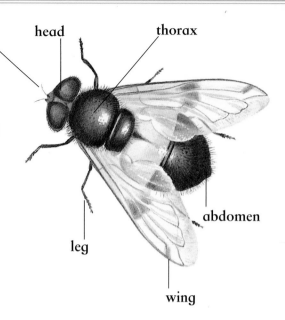

head
thorax
antenna
abdomen
leg
wing

 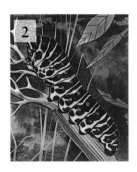  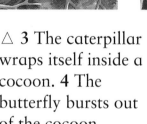

△ 1 A female butterfly lays eggs on a plant that her young will eat. A caterpillar hatches from each egg. 2 The caterpillar eats greedily and grows quickly.

△ 3 The caterpillar wraps itself inside a cocoon. 4 The butterfly bursts out of the cocoon.

adult swallowtail butterfly

potter wasp

◁ A female potter wasp makes a clay pot for each of her eggs. She puts live caterpillars into each pot, so that the baby wasp has food when it hatches.

△ The dragonfly is the fastest insect. It flies over ponds, streams, and rivers hunting other insects to eat.

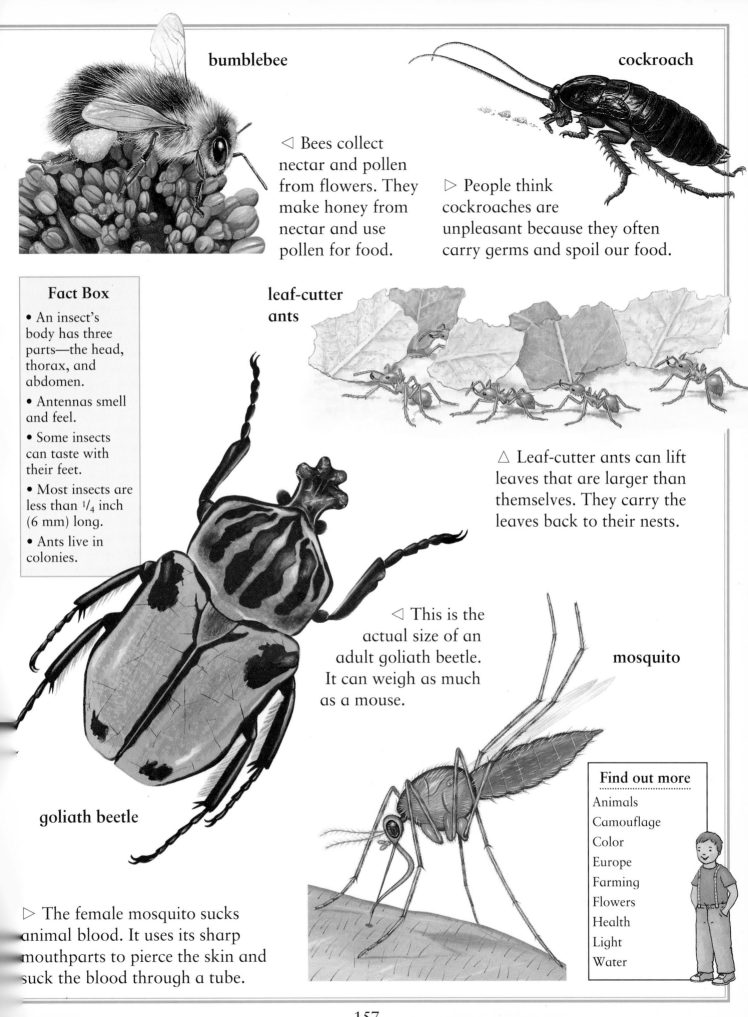

bumblebee

cockroach

◁ Bees collect nectar and pollen from flowers. They make honey from nectar and use pollen for food.

▷ People think cockroaches are unpleasant because they often carry germs and spoil our food.

leaf-cutter ants

Fact Box

• An insect's body has three parts—the head, thorax, and abdomen.

• Antennas smell and feel.

• Some insects can taste with their feet.

• Most insects are less than 1/4 inch (6 mm) long.

• Ants live in colonies.

△ Leaf-cutter ants can lift leaves that are larger than themselves. They carry the leaves back to their nests.

◁ This is the actual size of an adult goliath beetle. It can weigh as much as a mouse.

mosquito

goliath beetle

Find out more

Animals
Camouflage
Color
Europe
Farming
Flowers
Health
Light
Water

▷ The female mosquito sucks animal blood. It uses its sharp mouthparts to pierce the skin and suck the blood through a tube.

Inventions

Inventions are things that have been discovered or created so that we can do something better. Some inventions make it possible to do things we have not been able to do before. Many make life more comfortable or improve our health. Others have changed the way we travel, or given us new ways to speak to each other.

△ Long ago, people discovered it was easier to roll heavy things. So they invented the wheel.

wheel

refrigerator

△ A refrigerator keeps food and drink cool. Food stays fresher for longer. Before refrigerators were invented, people kept food cool with large blocks of ice.

▽ Plastic is made in factories from chemicals. It is a useful invention because it is easy to shape and it is tough. Lots of things are plastic.

▷ Television brings pictures and sounds from all over the world into our homes. In the United States people watch around 50 hours of TV a week.

television

▽ An incubator is a warm, closed bassinet. It protects sick babies and ones who are born early. They stay there until they are strong and well.

incubator

▷ This is a very old telescope. It was built by Galileo, a famous astronomer. An astronomer studies the stars and planets.

telescope

▽ Using a camera to take photographs is an easy way to keep a record of people, places, and events you have seen.

camera

▽ The invention of the telephone makes it possible for you to talk to someone else almost anywhere in the world.

telephone

Find out more

Bikes
Books
Cars
Computers
Flying machines
Trains
Space exploration

Jobs

People do all sorts of jobs. They may farm or fish. They may make things that others will sell. They may build homes, drive trucks, or look after sick people. People work mainly to earn money and may have several jobs during their lifetime.

△ Teachers work in schools. They help children to learn the things they need to know.

△ Farming is an important job all over the world. This man is cutting sugarcane.

△ Many people work in offices. They use computers to help them.

△ Supermarkets provide jobs. This man is arranging food on the shelves.

▷ It takes a lot of people to make a movie. These include actors, directors, people to record sound, and others to use the cameras.

Find out more
Books
Computers
Farming

160

Kangaroo and Wallaby

Kangaroos and wallabies live in Australia. They are marsupials. This means that the females have pouches on their bellies where their babies can grow until they are big enough to come out into the world.

▷ A baby kangaroo is called a "joey." When it is born, the baby is less than an inch long. It crawls up to the mother's pouch along a path the mother licks in her fur. Once in the pouch, the joey clings to a nipple and stays there until it is able to take care of itself.

△ There are 56 species of kangaroo and wallaby (the name given to the smaller kangaroos). Most live on the ground, but some live in trees.

▷ Kangaroos are excellent jumpers. They bound along on their strong back legs, using their long tails for balance. They can jump over 30 feet in one leap.

Find out more
Koala, Wombat, and Opossum
Mammal
Platypus

Killer whale

Killer whales are the largest members of the dolphin family. They are powerful hunters and can be up to 33 feet in length. Killer whales have strong jaws and teeth. They eat fish, dolphins, seals—even other whales.

▽ Killer whales find their way and track their prey by sending out little clicks of sound, then picking up the echo. They live in families called pods. Usually there are ten or so in a pod, but there may be up to 100. Like all whales, killer whales are mammals and give birth to live young.

Fact box
• Killer whales sometimes launch themselves onto a beach to catch seals resting near the water line.
• One killer whale caught in the Bering Sea had 32 seals in its stomach.
• Killer whales have never killed, or even attacked, humans.

△ Killer whales are fast swimmers, with rounded flippers and strong tails. They can swim at over 37 miles per hour, and can jump high out of the water. They live in most of the world's oceans, near the North and South poles.

Find out more
Dolphin
Shark

Koala, Wombat, and Opossum

Koalas live in the eucalyptus forests of eastern Australia. Because they look a little like bears, they are sometimes called koala bears. However, they are marsupials, not bears. Wombats and opossums are also marsupials.

△ Wombats look like koalas, and also live in Australia. But they are larger—between 28 and 48 inches long—and live on the ground. During the day they stay in the grassy nests that they make at the end of their long burrows. They come out at night to feed on grasses and the roots of shrubs and trees.

▽ The only marsupials to live outside Australia are opossums, which are found in North and South America. A typical opossum grows to about 40 inches long. At least half its length is its hairless tail, which can grip things.

△ When a young koala leaves its mother's pouch, it rides on her back. Koalas spend all their lives up in eucalyptus trees eating the leaves and bark. They only come down to cross to another clump of trees.

Find out more
Kangaroo and Wallaby
Mammal
Platypus

Light and Lenses

Without light we could not see anything. During the day, most of the light we see comes from the Sun. At night, we have artifical lights inside our homes and on the streets outside. Light usually travels in straight lines called rays. We see things because the rays hit an object, then bounce back into our eyes.

▷ Light from the Sun and lightbulbs is called white light. It is made up of different colors mixed together. Things look colored because they only reflect (bounce back) some of these colors and not others.

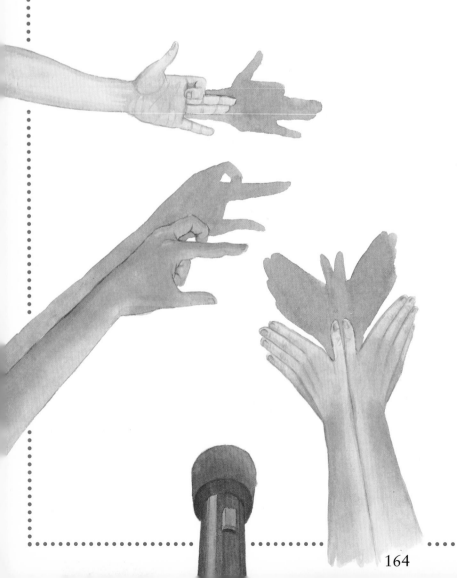

◁ Light travels in straight lines called rays. If the rays cannot reach a surface because there is something stopping them, a shadow forms. Your hand makes a shadow on the wall because it stops the light from reaching the wall.

▷ Light rays can be bent or made to change direction. When you put a straw into a glass, it looks bent. This is because the rays of light reflected from the straw bend when they leave the water and pass into the air.

Fact box
• Light travels at 187,000 miles per second. It takes eight minutes for rays of sunlight to get from the Sun to the Earth.

▽ This desert traveler can see a welcome pool of water in front of the palm trees. But the water is not really there. This is called a mirage. It happens when layers of warm air near the ground bend rays of light from the bright sky.

△ Like sunlight, the light from this flashlight is a mix of many colors. When the girl shines the flashlight on the green balloon, the balloon soaks up all the colors in the light, except green. Green light bounces back into the girl's eyes and she sees a green balloon.

◁ Some creatures, such as this glow worm, can produce light from their own bodies. The light is not to help the glow worm see. It is to attract a mate.

◁ A magnifying glass makes things look bigger. It does this by bending the straight rays of light as they pass through the glass lens.

▽ A telescope makes objects in the distance look larger. If you point a telescope at the night sky, you can see many more stars than you can with your eyes alone. This is because the telescope collects a lot more light than your eyes can collect.

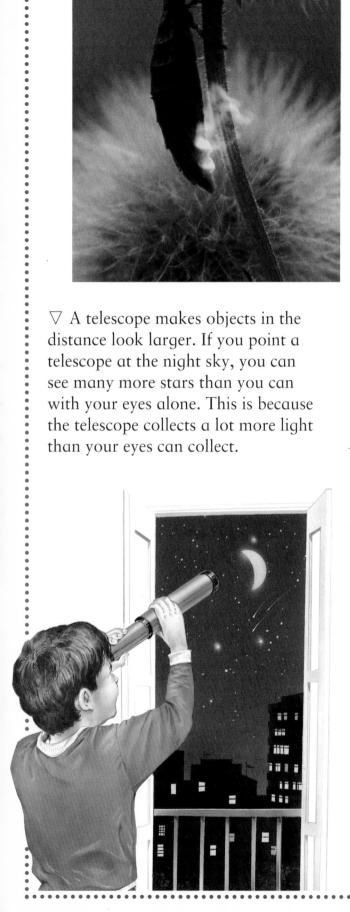

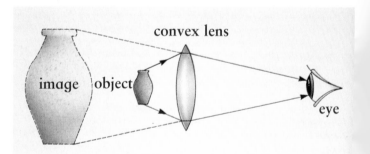

convex lens

image | object

eye

△ A magnifying glass works like this. When rays of light pass through the lens, they are bent inward, toward each other. When they reach your eye they seem to be coming from a much larger object.

convex lens

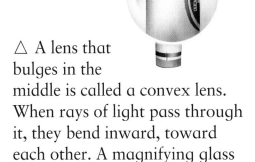

concave lens

△ A lens that bulges in the middle is called a convex lens. When rays of light pass through it, they bend inward, toward each other. A magnifying glass has a convex lens.

▽ A lens that is thinner in the middle is called a concave lens. Rays of light passing through it spread outward. If you look at something through a concave lens, it often looks smaller than it really is.

▷ A microscope makes things look much bigger than a magnifying glass does. It has lots of lenses inside, and can make things look hundreds of times bigger than they really are. This scientist is using a microscope to examine some of the tiny living things that cause disease.

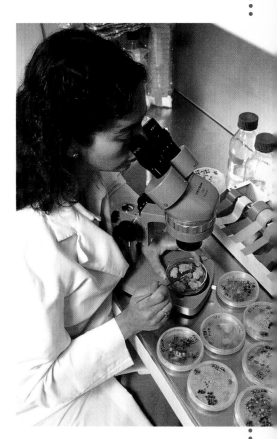

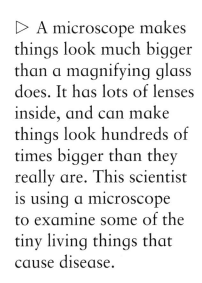

◁ With some people, the rays of light passing into their eyes do not bend enough to make a clear picture. With others, the rays may bend too much. The lenses in eyeglasses help people to see more clearly by correcting the amount the rays are bent.

Find out more
Color
Day and Night
Energy
Mirrors
Senses
Television

Lion

Lions are the largest predators in Africa. These powerful big cats live in groups called prides in bush country or on grassy plains. A pride is made up of several females and their cubs, as well as a few males. Except for humans, the lion has no enemies and is known as the "king of the beasts."

▽ Lions hunt mostly at night and spend the day resting. They prey on many of the large animals of the plains, including antelope, zebra, and buffalo. Besides caring for the cubs, the lionesses (female lions) do most of the hunting.

△ The male lion has a large, shaggy mane around its neck. It is his job to defend the territory of his pride, and he will warn off intruders with a loud roar. Adult lions have tawny coats, but lion cubs have spots.

Find out more
Cheetah
Mammal
Tiger

Living things

A living thing grows, feeds, breathes, and can reproduce (make young). The two main types of living things are plants and animals. Animals are living things that can move around. They eat other living things as food. Plants are living things that stay in one place. They make their own food using the energy from sunlight.

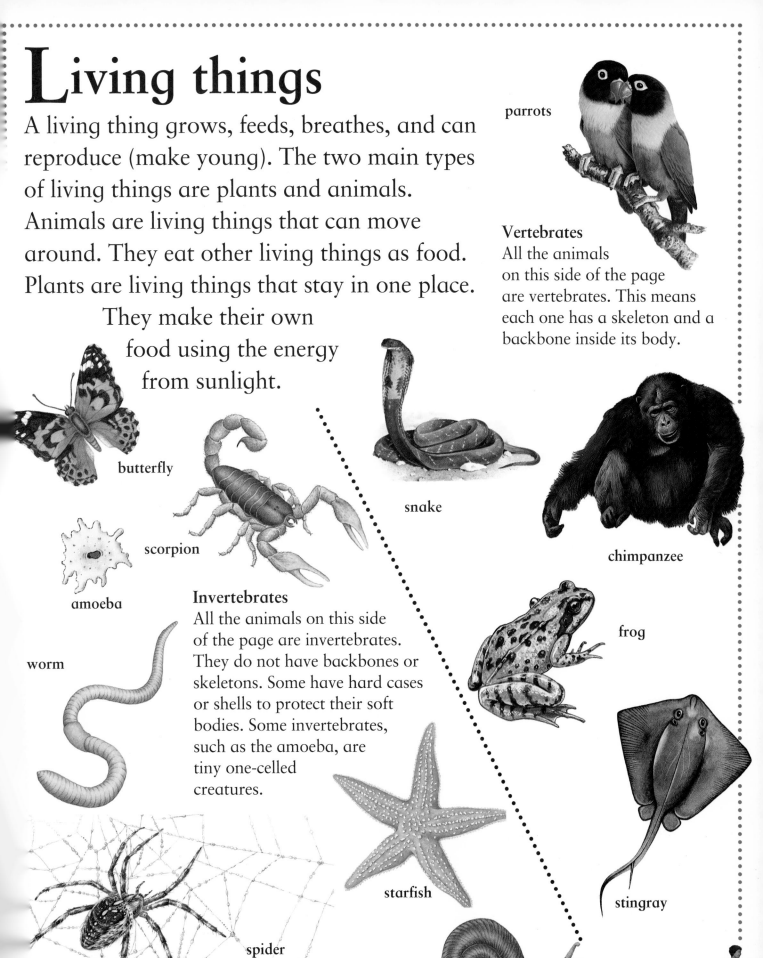

parrots

Vertebrates
All the animals on this side of the page are vertebrates. This means each one has a skeleton and a backbone inside its body.

butterfly

scorpion

snake

chimpanzee

amoeba

Invertebrates
All the animals on this side of the page are invertebrates. They do not have backbones or skeletons. Some have hard cases or shells to protect their soft bodies. Some invertebrates, such as the amoeba, are tiny one-celled creatures.

worm

frog

stingray

starfish

spider

snail

▽ Plants use energy from sunlight, and water and minerals from the soil to make their own food. Many plants make flowers seeds. The seeds grow into new plants.

flower

stem

leaf

root

△ Some animals, such as this bear, hibernate in the winter. This means that they go into a kind of deep sleep. This saves energy, as they do not need to hunt for food.

▽ Sea anemones look like plants but are really animals. They use their tentacles to catch small creatures to eat.

▽ There are hundreds of thousands of different kinds of plants. Some are so tiny that you can only see them through a microscope. Others, such as trees, can be huge.

△ Animals must find food to eat, or they will die. Some animals eat plants. Others, like this fish eagle, eat animals. Some animals, such as humans, eat both plants and animals.

Habitats

Arctic

desert

rain forest

grassy plain

▽ Dodos were a kind of bird that lived on a small island in the Indian Ocean. People killed so many for food that now there are no dodos left at all. They are extinct.

◁ Rhinoceroses are in danger of becoming extinct (dying out). One reason for this is because so many have been killed by hunters for their precious horns. This rhinoceros's horns have been cut off, to protect it.

◁ The places where plants and animals live are called their habitats. Animals and plants are usually specially suited to their particular habitats. Arctic animals have thick coats to keep them warm in the icy cold. Desert plants and animals need very little water to stay alive.

◁ Rain forests are home to about half of all the types of plants and animals in the world. In the grassy plains of Africa, hunters, such as lions, lie in wait to prey on antelopes and zebras.

Find out more
Air and Atmosphere
Day and Night
Earth
Human body
Medicine
Senses
Water

Lizard

Lizards are reptiles. They have scaly skin, long tails, and usually live in warm countries. Although they can dart around very quickly, they are cold-blooded and need to lie in the sun to keep warm.

△ The Gila monster is a lizard that lives in the North American deserts. Bright red-and-black markings warn that it has a poisonous bite.

△ Many lizards turn darker when basking in the sun. This helps their bodies absorb its heat better.

△ The Australian thorny devil looks frightening, but it is harmless. Its sharp spines save it from being eaten by predators.

◁ The frilled lizard of Australia lifts up its huge neck collar to scare off attackers.

Fact box

• The smallest lizards, the geckos of the Virgin Islands, are 1.5 inches long.
• If some species of lizard are caught by the tail, the tail breaks off. A new one will grow in its place within eight months.

Find out more
Chameleon

Llama

The llama is found in the high Andes mountains and on the dry plains of South America. Like its relative, the alpaca, it is tame. They are both relatives of the wild guanaco. All three are members of the camel family.

△ Guanacos usually live on mountains over 13,000 feet high, although they are also found on the lower plains. Their blood is rich in red cells, which helps them breathe the thin mountain air.

△ Today, llamas are used mainly as pack animals, as they were by the ancient Inca people of Peru. Female llamas are used for meat, but males are too tough to eat.

▷ Alpaca wool is prized by the local South American people. It has a soft feel and provides warmth in the cold climate.

Find out more
Camel
Goat
Mammal
Yak

Machines

Machines are things that make jobs easier and quicker to do. Some machines are very simple. For example, a hammer is a simple machine—so is a wheelbarrow, and so is a pair of scissors. People have used simple machines like these for thousands of years.

▽ **1** Make and use a simple machine. Start by putting some heavy books on a table. Try lifting them with your finger. It's hard work. Next, slide one end of a ruler under the books.

1

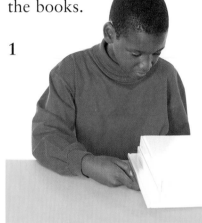

△ A slope does not look much like a machine. But it can be used as one because it makes getting to a high point easier than climbing straight upward.

▷ **2** Lift up the end of the ruler. This makes the books much easier to move. The ruler is working as a machine called a lever. We often use levers to help us lift things.

2

pliers

▽ Many of the machines we use at home need electricity to make them work.

wheelbarrow

◁ Pliers, a wheelbarrow, and a can opener are all examples of levers. When you push or pull one part of a lever, such as the pliers' handles, you make a push or pull on another part, such as the pliers' tips.

can opener

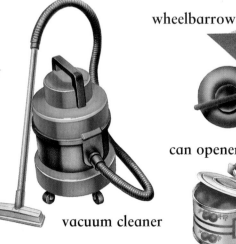

hairdryer

vacuum cleaner

◁ A pulley is a machine that helps you to lift heavy objects. It is made of a rope that runs around one or more wheels. As you pull down on one end of the rope, the other end rises and lifts whatever is attached to it.

△ A combine harvester is a complicated machine made of several machines rolled into one. It cuts the corn and threshes it, to get the grain from the straw (stems). Then it packs the straw into bales.

▷ Cars, aircraft, and trains are all transportation machines that move people and goods from place to place. They all have engines that turn fuel into energy, to turn their wheels or make them fly.

◁ A bicycle is made up of many simple machines that work together. For example, the pedals and gears are simple machines that make pedaling easier. The brakes are simple machines to help slow the wheels down.

Find out more
Energy
Engines
Force
Technology

Magnets

Have you ever tried to pick up a piece of paper with a magnet? It can't be done! Magnets can only pick up things made from certain kinds of metals. The most common of these are iron and steel. The force or pull that magnets exert is called magnetic force.

△ The area around a magnet is called its magnetic field. This is as far as its power stretches. To see a magnetic field, put a magnet on a sheet of paper and sprinkle some iron filings around it. The filings cluster inside the magnetic field, around the magnet's poles (ends).

fridge magnet

▽ One end of the magnet is called its north pole and the other is its south pole. Two north poles facing each other push each other apart. So do two south poles facing each other. But if a north pole faces a south pole, they pull towards each other.

fridge magnet

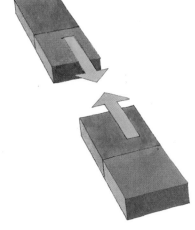

◁ The needle in a compass is actually a magnet. It swings around until its north pole points north—toward the Earth's magnetic north pole.

△ The Earth has its own magnetic field. It is as if the Earth has a huge bar-shaped magnet running through it, with its poles near the Earth's North and South poles.

the Earth's magnetic field

Fact box
• The biggest electromagnets weigh over 7,000 tons. That is as much as a thousand elephants!

▽ This train travels by floating along, just above a rail. There is a magnet inside the train and the rail is a magnet, too. The two magnets are arranged so that they push each other away. Because of this, the train floats above the rail as it moves.

◁ Make some fish from tinfoil. Fix a paperclip to each one. Make two toy fishing rods by tying magnets to pieces of string. Have a competition with a friend. Dangle the rods above the fish. Who catches the most?

1

◁ **1** You can make a magnet using electricity. This kind of magnet is called an electromagnet. You need some thin plastic-covered wire, a steel nail, and a flashlight battery. Start by winding the wire around the nail. Wind all the way up and down the nail until the wire is about three layers thick.

fridge magnet

2

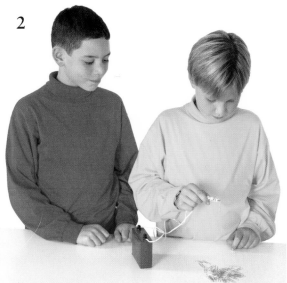

▷ **2** Fix one end of the wire to the top of the battery and the other end to the bottom, so that you have made a circuit. Now try picking up a paperclip or a steel thumbtack with the nail. What happens when you disconnect the battery?

Find out more
Battery
Earth
Electricity
Force
Machines
Materials
Recording
Television

Mammals

Mammals are vertebrate animals. They are warm-blooded and have body hair. Most give birth to live babies, not eggs that hatch later. Young mammals can drink their mother's milk.

The biggest mammal is the blue whale. It is about 100 feet (31 m) long and weighs more than 100 tons.

rabbit

△ A rabbit gives birth to lots of babies at the same time. A mother rabbit cares for her young until they can look after themselves.

humans

◁ Humans are mammals, too. We give birth to live babies. Humans depend on their parents for a long time.

▷ A kangaroo is a marsupial, which is a mammal that carries its young in a pouch. A baby kangaroo is called a joey.

kangaroo

lion

▷ Lions live in family groups called prides. They are good hunters and eat meat. A lioness cares for her cubs and teaches them how to hunt.

cubs

mole

▽ A mole is a burrowing mammal. It has strong front legs and big claws. These are for digging holes called burrows.

dolphins

bat

◁ Dolphins are mammals that live all their lives in the sea. Unlike fish, they have to come to the surface to breathe air.

△ Bats are the only mammals that can fly. A bat has a furry body. Its wings are soft, smooth skin.

chimpanzees

▽ The duck-billed Australian platypus is an unusual mammal because it lays eggs and does not give birth to live young animals.

duck-billed platypus

△ Chimpanzees live in family groups. They often comb each other's hair with their fingers. They also pick off dirt and insects.

Etruscan shrew

lioness

△ The tiny Etruscan shrew weighs no more than a large sugar cube.

Find out more
....
Animals
Australia and the Pacific Islands
Babies
Caves
Grasslands
Human body
Prehistoric life

Materials

Look around your classroom. Can you see clothes, shoes, chairs, tables, and books? What are these things made of? Some are made of plastic, and others are made of metal, wood, or fabrics. These are all materials. Different materials have different uses. For example, shoes are often made from leather or plastic because these are strong but will bend.

▷ These things are made from clay. Clay is a kind of soft earth that can be formed into different shapes. When it is baked it becomes very hard. Things made from clay are called ceramics.

Make a kite

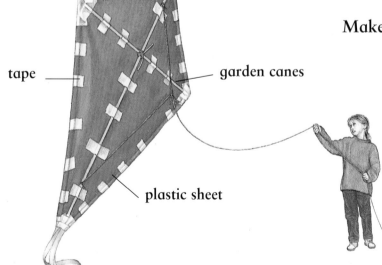

tape

garden canes

plastic sheet

ribbons

◁ What sort of materials would you use to make a kite like this one? Remember, a kite must be made of something light, so it will fly. It must be strong, so that it does not tear in the wind.

△ This kite's frame is made from thin garden canes. It is covered with sheets of plastic. The flying line is light, strong fishing line.

Meerkat

Meerkats are small meat-eating mammals. The word meerkat means "marsh cat." However, they actually live on the dry, open plains of Africa, not on marshes. They are known for their comic way of standing on their hind legs, on the lookout for predators.

△ Meerkats live in burrows under the ground. They come out during the day to hunt for food, but they are always watching out for eagles and other birds of prey.

▽ Meerkats often hunt by digging for prey with their long, sharp claws. They also look for insects, eggs, small animals, and plant roots to eat. They have a good sense of smell, and can see and hear well.

△ Like the meerkat, the mongoose will often attack poisonous snakes, in order to defend its burrow and its young.

Find out more
Cat (wild)
Cobra
Mammal

Melting and Boiling

Melting is when a solid turns into a liquid. Boiling turns liquid into a gas. These are called changes of state because they change a substance from one state of matter to another. A substance needs heat to make it melt or boil. There are two other changes of state. When gases cool, they may condense and become liquid. Liquids can be turned into solids by cooling or freezing.

△ What happens if you don't eat your Popsicle quickly enough? It melts in the warm air. The solid ice turns to liquid.

Warning! Never touch or move anything with hot or boiling liquid in it. You could get badly burned.

△ This beaker is full of nitrogen. Nitrogen is normally a gas, but if it is made very cold it condenses and turns into a liquid. In this picture, you can see it turning back into a gas in the warm air.

△ When you heat water, it gets hotter and hotter until the temperature reaches 212°F (100°C). It then boils and starts to turn into a gas called water vapor.

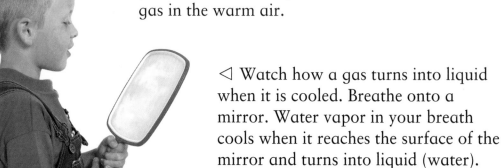

◁ Watch how a gas turns into liquid when it is cooled. Breathe onto a mirror. Water vapor in your breath cools when it reaches the surface of the mirror and turns into liquid (water).

Find out more
Energy
Gases
Solids

186

Metals

Most metals are hard, shiny materials. They can be bent or hammered into different shapes. Iron, copper, and aluminum are three kinds of metal. Most metals come from ores, which are a mixture of metal and rock. The ore is dug out of the ground. Different metals can be mixed to make tough, new metals, called alloys.

△ Aluminum is used to make foil, cans, and pipes; copper is used for pots and pans; steel for scissors and paperclips. Gold and silver are used to make jewelry.

▽ Iron becomes rusty if it is left in damp air. Rusty metal is weak and crumbles away. Metal things are often specially treated to prevent rust.

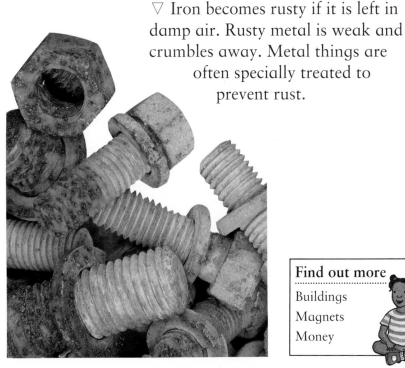

△ Iron ore is heated in a furnace. When it gets very hot, the iron melts. The iron is poured off, leaving the unwanted rock behind. The iron is then used to make steel.

Find out more

Buildings
Magnets
Money

Microscopic animal

Some animals are so tiny they can only be seen through a microscope. They live almost everywhere—in the water, in the air, in the ground, and even in your bed.

△ A good way to see microscopic animals is to look at pondwater through a microscope. Make a note of what you see as you look at the slide. You will probably see animals called daphnias, also known as water fleas.

Fact box
- There can be 5,000 house-dust mites on one speck of dust.
- Many people have tiny demodex mites living on their eyelashes.
- Some species of feather-winged beetle are as small as $1/1000$ inch in length.

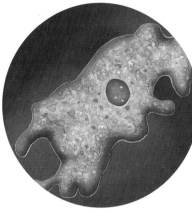

△ Amoebas are among the tiniest living things. They move by changing shape.

▷ Zooplankton are tiny creatures that drift in water. They are the food of the world's biggest animal, the blue whale.

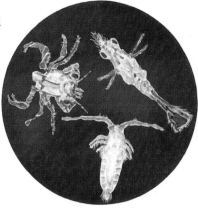

◁ House-dust mites are invisible to the naked eye. They feed on flakes of skin that they find in bedding and soft fabrics. These eight-legged creatures are related to spiders, and there are millions of them in each house.

Find out more
Beetle
Reproduction
Spider

Microwaves

Do you have a microwave oven in your kitchen? Microwaves are used in cooking, but they can also carry messages and signals through air and space. Satellite television programs are carried by microwaves. When you make an international telephone call, microwaves may carry the call up to a communications satellite in space, and then back down to Earth.

△ The dishes at the top of this tower send and pick up microwaves. These carry long-distance telephone calls.

Never put anything in a microwave oven without asking an adult first.

▷ There is a machine inside the oven that makes the microwaves.

▽ This is a microwave oven. Microwaves are beamed into the food. They make the atoms in the food move around. When this happens, the food gets hot and cooks.

fan

microwaves

◁ A fan scatters the microwaves around so that they reach every part of the food being cooked.

▷ Ships and aircraft use radar to detect objects around them. A radar dish sends out beams of microwaves. If these strike an object, they bounce back to the dish and the object shows up on a screen linked to the dish.

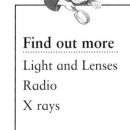

Find out more
Light and Lenses
Radio
X rays

189

Migration

Many animals make journeys from one place to another to find better living conditions. Some move fairly short distances, but others travel from one side of the world to the other. These regular return trips are known as migration.

▷ In the fall, you may see "V" formations of Canada geese flying overhead. Make a note of when they leave and in which direction they go. Watch for their return in the spring.

▽ The Earth is crisscrossed with animal migration routes. Use the color-keyed arrows on the map to see where these four migrating species travel each year.

■ Canada geese (above) fly to the Arctic Circle in the spring to breed. In the fall, they return to warmer southern regions.

■ Gray whales spend the winter in the warm sea off California, where they give birth to their calves. In the summer, they swim north to the rich food supplies in Alaskan waters.

■ Arctic terns travel farther than any other animal. Each year, they move from pole to pole and back again.

■ Swifts spend the summer in Europe, where they catch insects to feed their young. They spend the winter in Africa.

◁ Many grass-eating animals in Africa migrate to find food. Like these wildebeest, they follow the rain as it moves.

Find out more

Arctic tern
Reindeer

Mirrors

A mirror is a smooth, shiny surface that reflects nearly all the light that hits it. You can see yourself in a mirror because light reflects from you to the mirror and then bounces off the mirror and back into your eyes. Most mirrors are made of glass. Mirrors are not simply for looking at yourself. They have many other uses, too.

△ The back of a mirror is painted silver. Light bounces off this smooth layer of silver paint and into your eyes.

◁ How many other shiny surfaces can you find? Metals are very shiny. Other very smooth things, such as china plates, are shiny, too.

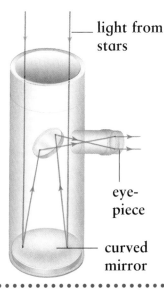

▷ Astronomers use large, powerful telescopes to look at the stars. These have mirrors inside them. The mirrors are curved like shallow dishes. They work in the same sort of way as lenses, to make things look nearer.

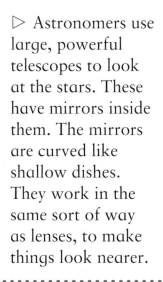

light from stars

eye-piece

curved mirror

△ Look at your reflection in a mirror. The mirror reflects your image straight out again so everything looks backwards. See if you can work out how this happens.

Find out more
Light and Lenses

191

Mole

Moles are small mammals that spend almost all their lives underground. We know they are around because of the molehills they create when digging their tunnels. They live in Europe, Asia, and North America.

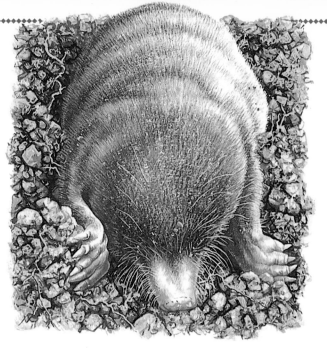

△ Big, powerful front paws, a pointed nose, and sharp claws mean that moles are excellent diggers. Although they have bad eyesight, they hunt for worms and insects by using their good sense of smell and by picking up vibrations with their whiskers.

△ Baby moles are born in a nest, called a fortress, deep below a molehill. They are lucky to be born at all—like all moles, their parents fought furiously when they first met.

◁ When moles dig tunnels they push the soil to the surface, which makes molehills. These are more common in the fall, when young moles look for new areas to live.

Fact box
• Moles surface at night to search for nest material.
• The star-nosed mole has a star of sensitive fleshy tentacles on its nose.
• People used to make clothes from mole fur.

◁ Golden moles are found in dry places in Africa. They live underground and burrow through sand to find food. Like all moles, they have very soft and silky coats.

Find out more
Badger
Mammal
Mouse

Money

Money is used to pay for the things we want to buy. Coins and paper bills are money. Each coin and bill is worth a different amount. People use bills for large amounts. Bills are printed on special paper and with complicated patterns that are hard to fake, or copy.

△ Before money existed, people exchanged the things they needed. This is called barter. The man on the left is bartering some cattle for armor.

▷ You can save your coins in a piggy bank. Put large amounts of money in a bank.

◁ Each country has its own type of money. The United States and Canada use dollars, Great Britain uses pounds, and France uses francs.

Find out more
Jobs
Metal

Monkey

Monkeys are intelligent mammals that can solve problems and hold things in their hands. They live in groups called troops, high in the tropical forests of the Americas, Africa, and Asia. Monkeys eat plants, birds' eggs, small animals, and insects.

△ A monkey's eyes face forward, which helps it see well when hunting. Most monkeys hunt by day.

▷ The capuchin monkey is a small monkey that lives in the Amazon jungle. Because of its intelligence and curious nature, many have been kept as pets and taught to do tricks.

△ Howler monkeys come from South America and are good climbers. They use their tails as an extra "hand" when swinging through the branches. Howler monkeys live in groups headed by an old male. They get their name from the loud calls the group makes together to warn other monkeys off their territory.

▽ The proboscis monkey of Borneo gets its name from its big nose. It has a long tail too, but uses it only for balance.

Fact box

• One difference between monkeys and apes is that monkeys have tails, while apes do not.
• A female monkey usually has one baby, or sometimes, twins.

Find out more
Baboon
Chimpanzee
Gorilla
Orangutan

Moon

The Moon is our closest neighbor in space. It is a large ball of dusty rock with no air, water, wind, or weather. No animals or plants can live there. Daytime on the Moon is boiling hot, but at night it is very cold. The Moon looks bright in the sky because it reflects light from the Sun.

▽ The Moon moves around the Earth once every month. Its path is called an orbit.

△ The Moon is covered with dents called craters. These were made when meteoroids crashed into the Moon. Meteoroids are large lumps of rock and metal.

Full Moon

△ There is a Full Moon once a month. The Sun shines on part of the Moon, and as the Moon orbits the earth its shape seems to change.

▽ On July 20, 1969, two American astronauts were the first people to set foot on the Moon. They were Neil Armstrong and Buzz Aldrin.

Find out more

Planets

Space exploration

Motion

Motion is another word for movement. Things cannot start to move on their own. They need a force (a push or a pull) to get them started. Once something has started to move, a force can make it move faster, or it can slow it down again. Speeding up motion is called acceleration. Slowing it down is called deceleration.

△ This shot-putter uses force to get the shot moving through the air. Gravity pulls at the shot as it travels along. It slows the shot down and then pulls it back to the ground.

◁ **1** A moving object will always try to keep moving, and a still object will try to stay still. This is called inertia. Try this experiment. Put a raw egg on a tray and spin it. As the egg spins, the runny yolk inside it spins, too.

▷ **2** Stop the egg, then quickly let go of it. It starts to spin again. This is because the yoke inside the egg has inertia. It goes on moving when you stop the shell. When you let go of the shell, inertia starts the egg moving again.

Fact box
• People used to try to make machines called perpetual motion machines, that would keep on moving forever. None of these machines ever worked because friction always made them stop.

△ The faster a car is going, the longer it takes for it to stop. That is why it is important for drivers to go slowly in places where people may be crossing the street.

△ These heavy railroad cars need a lot of force to make them move. The locomotives had to exert a huge pull on them to get them started. Heavy things are harder to get moving and harder to slow down than light things.

▷ Moving objects always try to keep going in a straight line. The boy is swinging the weight on the end of this string in a circle. The weight needs a force to keep it moving in a circle. The force comes from the string. Without it, the weight would fly off in a straight line.

▽ A grasshopper is light and small. Its legs give a huge push compared to its size, which helps it to accelerate very fast when it hops away.

Find out more
Energy
Flight
Force

197

Mountains

A mountain is a very high hill—an area that is much higher than the land around it. Mountains have steep sides. They are often much colder at the top. Some of the highest peaks are covered in snow all year. Above a certain height, called the tree line, the climate is too harsh for trees to grow.

◁ Skiing is a fast way to get across snow. It is a popular mountain sport.

mountain goat

△ Mountain goats have thick, woolly coats and are good climbers.

trumpet gentian

△ Mountain plants grow in low clumps. This is to protect them from the cold winds.

Find out more

Asia

Europe

Oceans and seas

South America

Volcano

198

Mouse

Mice are small rodents with long tails and sharp front teeth. These grow all the time, so mice must gnaw things to stop them from getting too long. There are many kinds of wild mice, found all over the world. Mice can also be kept as pets.

△ Mice eat many foods, including seeds, grain, roots, fruit, and insects. They also enjoy human food. The house mouse lives in people's homes.

△ American harvest mice are good at climbing. They build globe-shaped nests above the ground on the stems of grasses.

▽ Test how smart your pet mouse is with this mouse-maze. Cut some cardboard into strips 6 inches wide, then glue the strips to a wooden board in a maze pattern. Put some food at the end of the maze and see how long your mouse takes to find it. Repeat to see if it gets quicker at solving the maze.

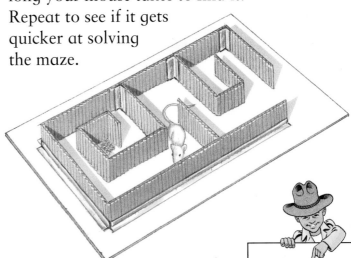

◁ Dormice live in Europe, Africa, and Asia. Unlike many other mice, they have furry tails. Dormice make nests from plants and, in cold places, sleep through the winter.

Find out more
Beaver
Food
Guinea pig, Gerbil, and Hamster
Rat

Music

There are many different kinds of music and most people like playing or listening to it. They may sing or play an instrument such as a piano or a guitar, by themselves or in a band or orchestra. People play music to celebrate special occasions, to entertain themselves or others, or just to relax. A person who plays an instrument is called a musician.

△ You probably listen to music on tapes, CDs, and records at home, or hear it on the radio and television.

△ An orchestra is a large group of musicians who play a variety of different instruments. Orchestras often play music for concerts, operas, ballets, or plays.

▷ At celebrations in the Caribbean islands, steel bands play in the streets or on the beach. The steel drums are made out of specially shaped, empty oil drums.

▷ This Japanese robot can play the keyboard much faster than a human can. It can read music or play a tune that is stored in its memory.

WABOT-2

▽ You can play music too. You may already play the piano or the recorder. There are many other kinds of musical instruments. These children are creating music with their instruments.

triangle

cymbal

tambourine

◁ Wolfgang Amadeus Mozart was one of the world's most famous musicians. He played in public when he was a child, and he wrote his first piece of music when he was only five years old.

Find out more

Australia

Dance

Sound

North America

North America is the world's third largest continent. In the north it is cold and there are large forests and many lakes. In the south there are hot deserts and thick rain forests. The middle is a huge area of flat grassland, called the prairies. The Rocky Mountains are in the western part of the continent. Many North Americans live in busy, modern cities.

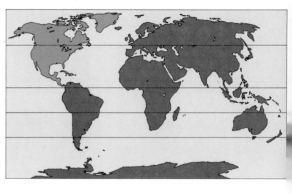

△ North America is shown in blue on this map. Most of it is covered by Canada, the United States, and Mexico.

◁ Many people visit Las Vegas, a city built in the middle of the desert. At night its brightly lit buildings shine against the dark sky.

△ People of many countries have come to live in North America. This picture shows some of the children and grandchildren of those people.

◁ A stall owner getting ready for market day in Oaxaca (Wah-**ha**-ka), in Mexico. Mexican farmers were the first people to grow chilies, tomatoes, avocados, corn, and many kinds of beans.

▷ There are billions of tiny plants and animals floating in the sea. They are called plankton. Many fish and other sea creatures feed on them.

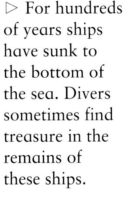
plankton

sperm whale

◁ Whales are the largest creatures in the ocean. This sperm whale can grow up to 65 feet (20 meters) long.

▽ An octopus has eight long arms. If an octopus loses an arm, it grows a new one.

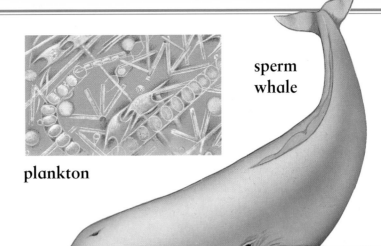

blue ringed octopus

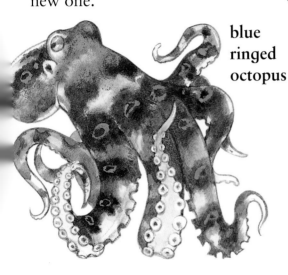

▷ For hundreds of years ships have sunk to the bottom of the sea. Divers sometimes find treasure in the remains of these ships.

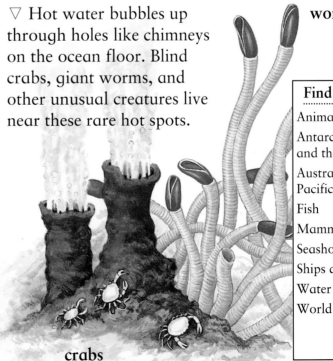

▽ Divers use small diving ships called submersibles to explore deep water. They go down to search for shipwrecks and to study ocean life.

submersible

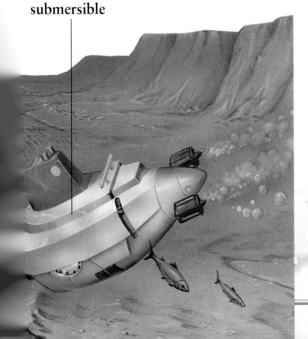

▽ Hot water bubbles up through holes like chimneys on the ocean floor. Blind crabs, giant worms, and other unusual creatures live near these rare hot spots.

worms

crabs

Find out more
....
Animals

Antarctica and the Arctic

Australia and the Pacific islands

Fish

Mammals

Seashore

Ships and boats

Water

World

Octopus and Squid

The octopus is a sea creature with eight long arms, called tentacles. These can wind around objects and have suckers on them that grip. The squid is related to the octopus, but it has ten arms.

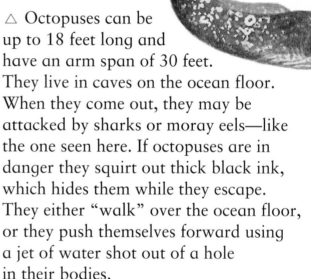

◁ Squid range in length from less than an inch right up to 65 feet for the largest species. Two of their ten arms are especially long and have suckers on the end.

△ Octopuses can be up to 18 feet long and have an arm span of 30 feet. They live in caves on the ocean floor. When they come out, they may be attacked by sharks or moray eels—like the one seen here. If octopuses are in danger they squirt out thick black ink, which hides them while they escape. They either "walk" over the ocean floor, or they push themselves forward using a jet of water shot out of a hole in their bodies.

◁ Octopuses ambush their prey, such as crabs, shellfish, and shrimp. Their tentacles draw the victim toward their powerful, birdlike beak. This is hidden at the base of the tentacles.

Find out more
Crab
Shellfish
Starfish

Orangutan

The word orangutan means "man of the forest" in the Malay language, and it is true that this large ape does look a little like an old, hairy man. Orangutans live in Southeast Asia.

Fact box

• Male orangutans weigh up to 200 pounds and may grow to be 5 feet tall.
• In the wild, orangutans live about 35 years.
• When it rains, orangutans often use a large leaf as an umbrella.

▷ Baby orangutans are reared by their mothers and will stay with them until they are around five years old.

△ Orangutans have become rare partly because their forest habitat has been cut down, but also because some people think baby orangutans make good pets, and steal them from the wild. Mothers are often killed while defending their babies.

▽ Orangutans have long, strong arms. They climb slowly through the trees in the morning and evening searching for wild figs—their favorite food. At night they sleep on platforms made of branches.

Find out more
Baboon
Chimpanzee
Gorilla
Monkey

Ostrich, Emu, and Cassowary

Not all birds can fly. Although they have small wings, the world's biggest birds—ostriches, cassowaries, and emus—can only walk and run.

▽ Emus are the second tallest birds, growing to 6 feet. They live on the grasslands of Australia.

△ Ostriches lay up to eight giant eggs in a nest on the ground. The male sits on the eggs at night; the female sits during the day.

▽ Male ostriches are black and white. They are the biggest birds of all—often 8 feet tall. Females are slightly smaller and grayish-brown. They can run at 40 miles per hour.

Fact box

- Ostriches live in Africa.
- Ostrich eggs are the biggest of all bird eggs.

◁ Cassowaries live in the forests of New Guinea and Australia. They are 5 feet tall and have featherless heads with a bony helmet on the top. If attacked, they will kick and slash with their clawed feet. Their middle toe is as sharp as a dagger.

Find out more

Bird

Otter

Otters are mammals found near rivers and seashores around the world. Although the otter makes its home on the land, it spends much of its time in the water.

△ Female otters give birth to between one and five young in an underground burrow called a holt.

▷ Otters eat fish and small animals. They are strong swimmers and well designed for hunting in the water.

long tail: this acts like as ship's rudder to steer the otter

fur: two layers keep the otter warm and dry

eyes and nose: on top of the head so the otter can see and breathe while swimming

whiskers: help the otter feel movements in the water

teeth: long, sharp teeth grip and bite prey and crack shells

feet: webbed feet for swimming fast

claws: sharp claws help the otter dig

▽ Young otters spend lots of time playing and wrestling with each other. One of their favorite games is to slide down a snow or mud bank.

△ Sea otters are found along the northern rim of the Pacific Ocean—from California to northern Japan. They often float on their backs and sometimes carry their young on their bellies.

Find out more
Beaver
Platypus
Seal and Sea lion

Owl

Owls are birds of prey that hunt mostly at night. They use their sensitive hearing and large eyes (which give them good night vision) to catch animals such as mice and rabbits. Owls have soft feathers that allow them to fly silently. The hooting cry of some species is easy to recognize.

△ Tawny owls were once found only in woodlands. Today, they also live in towns and cities, where they hunt mice and rats. During the day, they settle in the trees of parks and yards.

◁ The burrowing owls of North and South America live in burrows in the ground. They either dig a hole themselves or use one left by another animal, such as a gopher.

▽ Barn owls build nests in buildings, hollow trees, or old hawk's nests. The round, flat shape of the barn owl's head helps it hear its prey. Once it has caught the animal, the adult brings it to the chicks in the nest.

Fact box

• Owls can swivel their heads almost all the way around when they are listening for sounds.
• Snowy owls live in the Arctic. They mainly hunt lemmings. These owls nest on the ground.

Find out more
Bat
Birds
Eagle

Panda

The giant panda is a bear found in just a few high bamboo forests in China. There are probably no more than 1,500 giant pandas left in the wild. About 100 are kept in zoos around the world.

▽ Pandas have one or two cubs at a time. At birth, a cub weighs only 3.5 ounces. At first the mother holds it close to her chest at all times. But it grows quickly, and after ten weeks the cub starts to crawl.

△ Giant pandas usually eat only bamboo. To help them grasp the stems, they have an extra pad on their front paws that works like a thumb. Giant pandas have become rare since their forests have been cut down, and because they were once hunted for their fur.

▷ Red pandas look very much like raccoons. They live in the high forests of the Himalayas, from Nepal to China. They feed at night on roots, acorns, bamboo, and fruit.

Find out more
Bear
Mammal
Polar bear
Raccoon

Parrot

Parrots live in warm, tropical places around the world. They have strong, hooked beaks for cracking nuts and seeds. Each foot has two pairs of toes, which helps the birds perch and grip food.

▷ Macaws are brilliantly colored parrots from South America. They are large, noisy birds, and their piercing screams can often be heard in tropical rain forests.

△ Cockatoos are parrots found in Australia. This sulfur-crested cockatoo has a crest that it can raise and lower. Cockatoos are popular as pets, and often learn to copy human speech.

▷ Lovebirds are brightly-colored, small parrots from Africa and Madagascar. They get their name from the way they sit together in pairs, resting their heads against each other.

Find out more

Birds
Hummingbird
Peacock

Peacock

The peacock is one of the world's most beautiful birds. Peacocks first lived in Asia, but because of their colorful feathers, they have been kept in parks and gardens for thousands of years. They have a loud, piercing cry and eat snails, frogs, insects, and plants.

▽ Peacocks have shiny green or blue tail feathers, tipped with a pattern like an eye. To attract females, they raise their tails and vibrate them.

▽ The female is called a peahen. Peahens have short tails, and much duller feathers than the males.

Fact box

• Peacocks have the longest tail feathers of any bird—over 5 feet.
• In 1936, a hunt started for the African Congo peacock when a single feather was discovered. The bird itself was finally found 23 years later.

▽ Pheasants are members of the same family as peacocks. Male pheasants also have long, decorative tails and brightly patterned feathers. Pheasants originally came from the Far East, but have been bred in many countries for hunting.

Find out more

Birds
Chicken and Turkey

Pelican

There is a rhyme about the pelican —"its beak can hold more than its belly can"—and this is true. The pelican's beak has a huge pouch, which holds three times as much as its stomach. It uses the pouch to scoop up fish from the water.

▷ Pelicans bring fish back for their young in their throats. The baby pelicans reach down into the throat to take the fish.

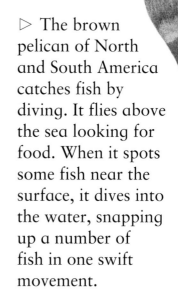

▷ The brown pelican of North and South America catches fish by diving. It flies above the sea looking for food. When it spots some fish near the surface, it dives into the water, snapping up a number of fish in one swift movement.

◁ American white pelicans use teamwork to catch fish. One group will guide the fish into shallow water by paddling their feet and moving their beaks. Once the fish are trapped, the other birds plunge their beaks in to scoop them up.

Find out more

Flamingo, Heron, and Stork

Penguin

Penguin

Penguins are seabirds that live in some of the world's coldest places. They are found on islands in the seas around Antarctica, and on the southern tips of South America, South Africa, and Australia. Penguins cannot fly, but they can swim better than any other bird.

△ Penguins swim using their small, stiff wings like flippers. Their tails and feet are used for steering. They hunt fish and krill, a type of shrimp. Waterproof feathers and layers of fat keep them warm.

△ Emperor penguins do not make nests. Instead, the male keeps the egg warm by balancing it on his feet. When the chick hatches, it huddles close to its parent's body for the first few weeks.

◁ The Adélie penguin of the Antarctic islands lives in big, noisy colonies. When calling to attract a mate or to warn off other penguins, they throw back their heads.

◁ While the emperor penguin (above) can be up to 4 feet tall, the smallest penguin is the fairy penguin, which reaches a height of just 16 inches.

Find out more

Baby animal
Ostrich, Emu, and Cassowary
Seal and Sea lion

Physics

Physics is the study of how the universe works, and how and why things happen in it. People who study physics are called physicists. They study things such as why objects move when they are pushed, how electricity works, and why things melt when they are heated. Some physicists try to find out what happens inside atoms and what the universe is made of.

△ Physicists make important discoveries. About 300 years ago, Italian scientist Galileo dropped objects from the Tower of Pisa to show that heavy things do not fall faster than light ones.

Mechanics This is the study of how things move.

mechanics

Electricity Physicists study how electricity works.

mechanics

sound

Optics Studying optics means finding out about light.

optics

optics

energy

Energy Physicists study how energy makes things happen.

electricity

Sound Physicists study how sound travels from place to place.

heat (and cold)

Heat Studying heat means finding out about melting, boiling, and how things get hot or cold.

Find out more
Light and Lenses
Melting and Boiling
Motion

Pig

Pigs were first tamed 9,000 years ago in China. Today most pigs are farm animals, raised for their meat and skins. Pigs eat almost anything. They are intelligent animals, and some people keep them as pets.

△ There are over 90 breeds of tame pig. They grow very quickly, and when raised on a special diet, may grow to 6.5 feet in length in just two years.

△▷ Baby pigs are called piglets. The mother pig, called a sow, usually has a litter of up to 12, and has two rows of nipples along her belly for them to drink milk from. Sometimes the weakest piglet, called a runt, is not able to feed and needs to be cared for by a human.

▽ Wild boars are fierce animals that live in forests in many countries. The piglets have striped coats that help camouflage them.

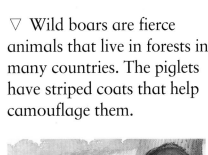

Find out more
Camouflage
Goat
Mammal

Planets

Planets are huge balls of rock, metal, and gas that travel around a star. The Earth is one of the nine planets that travel around our star, the Sun. The Sun, and all of the planets, moons, and lumps of rock, dust, and ice that whirl around it, make up our Solar System. The Earth only has one moon traveling around it, but some planets have several moons.

Sun

Earth

orbi

△ The planet travels around the Sun in paths called orbits. A complete orbit is called a year. For the earth this is just over 365 days.

Fact box

• Mercury is the planet closest to the Sun.

• Venus is the hottest planet. It is covered with thick clouds of poisonous gas.

• Earth is the only planet with air and water.

• Mars is a red, rocky planet. It is very dry and has dust storms.

Jupiter

Earth

Mercury

Mars

Venus

Sun

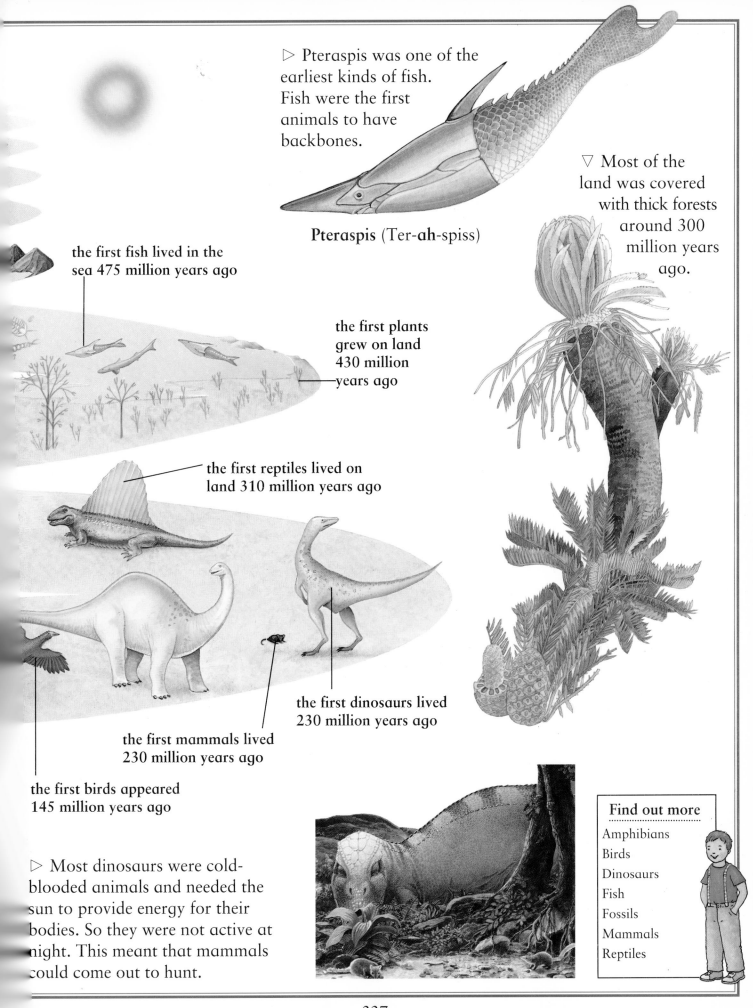

▷ Pteraspis was one of the earliest kinds of fish. Fish were the first animals to have backbones.

Pteraspis (Ter-**ah**-spiss)

▽ Most of the land was covered with thick forests around 300 million years ago.

the first fish lived in the sea 475 million years ago

the first plants grew on land 430 million years ago

the first reptiles lived on land 310 million years ago

the first dinosaurs lived 230 million years ago

the first mammals lived 230 million years ago

the first birds appeared 145 million years ago

▷ Most dinosaurs were cold-blooded animals and needed the sun to provide energy for their bodies. So they were not active at night. This meant that mammals could come out to hunt.

Find out more
Amphibians
Birds
Dinosaurs
Fish
Fossils
Mammals
Reptiles

Rabbit and Hare

Rabbits and hares are closely related. Hares are bigger than rabbits and have longer ears and legs. Hares live aboveground, while rabbits live underground in linked-up tunnels, called warrens.

△ The black-tailed jack rabbit of the hot North American deserts is really a hare. Its very long ears help it cool down in the fierce heat of the day.

△ Rabbits were originally found in the countries around the Mediterranean Sea. Humans have now introduced them throughout the world.

▽ Rabbits are popular pets. They are friendly animals and easy to keep in outdoor hutches. They need to be fed and given fresh water every day, and their hutches must be cleaned regularly.

Fact box

• Rabbits have up to ten babies in a litter and give birth seven times a year.
• Young hares are called leverets.
• Top speed for a hare is 35 miles per hour.

Find out more

Guinea pig, Gerbil, and Hamster
Rat
Squirrel

Raccoon

The striped tail and black mask of the North American raccoon make it easy to spot. Raccoons are forest creatures, but they have learned to scavenge from humans and often make their dens near towns.

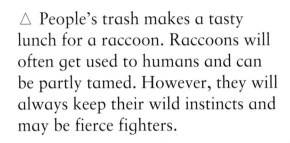

△ People's trash makes a tasty lunch for a raccoon. Raccoons will often get used to humans and can be partly tamed. However, they will always keep their wild instincts and may be fierce fighters.

Fact box

• The raccoon gets its name from a Native American word that means "scratches with hands."
• There are seven raccoon species.
• Wild raccoons live for about five years.

△ Even though they are weaned at two months, young raccoons are protected by their mother for up to a year.

▷ In the wild, raccoons eat berries, acorns, and seeds. They like to live near rivers so they can hunt for crabs, frogs, and fish. They will also rinse any dirty food in the water. When the young are old enough, they will leave their mother to live on their own.

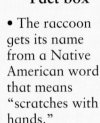

Find out more

Bear
Beaver
Fox
Panda

Radio

Radio is a way of sending messages over long distances. Sounds are turned into waves, called radio waves. These travel from one place to another through air and space. You cannot see them because they are invisible. Radio waves are also used to send signals from radio and television stations, and to carry messages to and from cellular telephones.

△ The antenna on a radio picks up radio waves coming from a transmitter. The radio turns the waves back into sound.

◁ In a radio station, music and other sounds are turned into an electrical signal. This signal goes to a transmitter, which turns it into radio waves.

▷ A walkie-talkie turns the sound of your voice into radio waves. The waves travel to another walkie-talkie which turns them back into sound.

△ This is a radio telescope. It picks up radio waves coming from space. Astronomers study these waves to find out things about the Universe that they cannot learn from ordinary telescopes.

Find out more

Electricity
Microwaves
Sound
Telephones

Rat

Rats are rodents with sharp teeth, furry bodies, and long tails. There are over 120 types of rat, living all over the world. The brown rat and the black rat are the most common.

△ Brown rats and black rats originally came from Asia, but they are now found all over the world, wherever humans live. It is said that there is probably one rat for every person on the planet.

△ Both black and brown female rats will have between six and 22 babies in a litter. They can have up to seven litters a year.

▷ Pack rats, also called wood rats, are American rodents that live in nests made of plants. They are nocturnal and eat grasses and cereals.

Fact box

• Rats can carry about 30 diseases affecting humans.
• In the Middle Ages, one in four Europeans died from the plague—a disease spread by rats.
• Rats have been known to gnaw through electric cables!

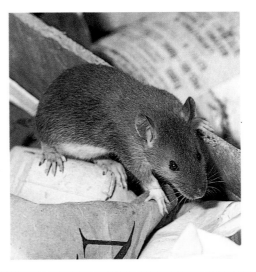

▷ Humans see rats as pests because they spread disease and spoil human foods. They are intelligent animals and will use their sharp teeth to bite through most obstacles.

Find out more

Beaver
Guinea pig, Gerbil, and Hamster
Mouse

231

Rattlesnake

Rattlesnakes are found in North and South America. They are named after their spooky rattle, which warns other animals that they are very poisonous. There are about 30 species of rattlesnake.

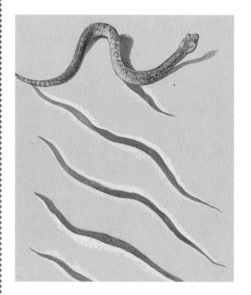

◁ The sidewinder is a rattlesnake that lives in sandy deserts in Mexico and the southwestern United States. Its unusual method of moving sideways leaves a distinctive trail.

△ Most rattlesnakes rest during the day and hunt small rodents at night. They detect prey by "tasting" the air for smells with their forked tongue. As the prey moves closer, the rattlesnake feels its body warmth with heat-sensitive pits on the sides of its face.

Fact box

• At 8 feet long, the eastern diamondback is the biggest rattlesnake.
• A rattlesnake's poison comes out of two fangs in its upper jaw.
• The bite of a rattlesnake can be deadly.

▷ Inside a rattlesnake's tail is a set of hard, loose pieces. It is these that produce the rattling noise. You can make your own rattle by threading some bottle tops onto a long nail and attaching it to a length of wood (get an adult to help you). You might scare a few people!

Find out more
Cobra
Reptile

Recording

Recording something means storing it in a way that makes it possible to see or hear it again and again. We can record voices, music, and pictures.

When we talk about recording, we usually mean recording sound. What we actually record are vibrations in the air. We can do this with a tape recorder.

△ 1 When you record your voice, a microphone turns sound (vibrations in the air) into an electrical signal. The signal is recorded on the tape in the tape recorder.

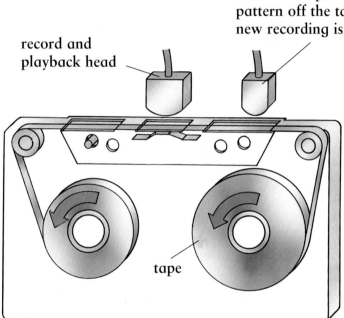

record and playback head

this head wipes the magnetic pattern off the tape before a new recording is made

tape

◁ 2 The tape in a tape recorder has a special magnetic coating. When a recording is being made, an electromagnet in the recorder makes an invisible pattern on the tape.

△3 To play a recording, the tape recorder turns the invisible patterns into an electrical signal. This signal goes to a loudspeaker, which turns it into sound.

▷ On a compact disc (CD), sounds are recorded as a pattern of tiny pits in the surface. A laser beam in the player reads this pattern and the electronics inside the player turn it into sound.

Fact box

• Many airplanes have flight recorders that record the airplane's movements during a flight. A cockpit voice recorder records what the pilots say during the flight as well.

Find out more
Electricity
Magnets
Sound
Video

Reindeer

Reindeer are found in the Arctic regions of Asia, Europe, and North America. They live on the tundra (plains) and in forests. The reindeer is closely related to the caribou of North America.

▽ Like all other deer, reindeer lose their antlers in the spring, then grow a new set that reaches full size in the fall. Reindeer are the only deer where the females have antlers as well as males.

△ Reindeer feed on grass, lichens, and twigs. In the winter they use their large hooves to shovel the snow away to dig for food. In the winter their thick coats are gray; in the summer they are brown.

▽ People first tamed the reindeer over 3,000 years ago, and they have been used as transportation and for their meat and fur ever since. Humans have never managed to tame the caribou.

◁ Reindeer and caribou migrate over long distances. They move south in the fall and north in the spring. Young or weak animals are often preyed on by hungry wolves.

Find out more
Deer
Elk
Mammal
Migration

234

Religion

There are many religions around the world and the people who follow them have different beliefs and customs. Most religions have a god or gods and have rules to help people to live with each other. People who follow a religion may meet together in a special building. They usually have someone, such as a priest, minister, or rabbi, to guide them. The most popular religions include Christianity, Islam, Judaism, Hinduism, Buddhism, and Sikhism.

church

△ Many people worship in special buildings. They may pray in a church, like this one, or a mosque, a temple, or a synagogue.

Christians
These Christians are celebrating Easter Sunday. They believe that Jesus, the Son of God, died on the cross and came back to life three days later. Easter celebrates his rising from the dead. His teachings are in the New Testament of the Bible.

Sikhs

Sikhs believe in one God and follow the teachings of gurus. They are taught to lead good, simple lives. The Golden Temple at Amritsar in India is the most important holy place where Sikhs go to pray.

Hindus

Hindus worship many gods and believe the soul is reborn after death. Every year Hindus celebrate Divali, the festival of lights, to bring good fortune.

Jews

Here the candles are being lit during the eight-day festival of Hanukkah. Jews believe in one God and their teachings and laws are written in the Bible.

green
turtle

◁ A turtle swims
using its strong
flippers. This turtle
lives in the sea,
but it lays its eggs
on the seashore.

▽ Many snakes have jaws that
stretch. They can open their mouths
very wide. Some snakes can
swallow a large animal whole.

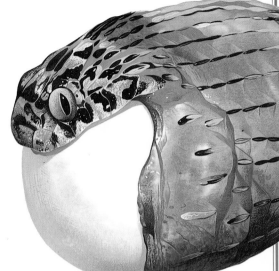

egg-eating snake

▷ The tortoise
lives on land. It
pulls its head and
legs into its shell
if it is scared.

tortoise

▽ The anaconda is a huge
snake from South America.
It coils its body around its
prey and squeezes it to death.

caiman

anaconda

▽ The Komodo dragon is the
largest lizard. It can grow up to
11½ feet (3.5 meters) long. It
attacks deer and pigs.

Komodo
dragon

Find out more
Animals
Dinosaurs
Prehistoric life

Rhinoceros

Rhinoceroses (or rhinos) are large, heavy animals that live on open grassland in Asia and Africa. They are protected from predators by tough, armored skin and sharp horns. Although rhino horn is very hard, it is actually made of a material similar to hair.

△ Rhinos weigh up to 5.5 tons and can charge at 30 miles per hour.

▽ Rhinos have poor eyesight, but a very good sense of smell. Females with young calves are likely to charge if they feel threatened by an unfamiliar sound or scent, and males are often bad-tempered. But rhinos will let birds called oxpeckers ride on their backs and feed on insects living on the rhino's skin.

Indian rhino   African white rhino   African black rhino

△ African rhinos have two horns; Asian rhinos have one. Indian rhinos have a long upper lip for eating reeds and grass. The white rhino, which is actually gray, has a wide upper lip for grazing. The black rhino uses its pointed upper lip to eat leaves.

Find out more

Elephant
Hippopotamus
Horse
Pig

Roads

Roads link one place to another. Cars, buses, and trucks travel on roads. There are special roads called highways or expressways, so that traffic can travel a long way without stopping. Signs and markings on roads tell drivers which way to go and how fast to travel.

△ Bridges and overpasses help traffic to travel more quickly around crowded cities. Some roads go underground, through tunnels.

How a road is made
▷ Bulldozers shovel away trees and earth.

bulldozer

◁ Scrapers make the ground level and smooth out a path. Scrapers are pulled by very large tractors.

scraper

dump truck

grader

◁ Dump trucks bring crushed rock. Graders smooth this in place to make a flat base for the road.

roller

paving machine

△ A paving machine spreads on a mixture of stones, sand, and tar, called asphalt. This is rolled flat.

Find out more
Conservation
Energy

243

Salmon and Trout

Salmon and some kinds of trout are found in the cold northern parts of the Atlantic and Pacific oceans. Most types of trout, however, live in fresh water. Large salmon can weigh over 65 pounds, while the largest trout weigh over 30 pounds.

△ There are many different types of trout. The brightly colored rainbow trout (above) is one of the most common. It was introduced to Europe from North America and people often catch it for sport.

▽ Before they breed, salmon migrate thousands of miles from their homes in the sea, back to the rivers where they were born. They battle upstream against strong currents, clearing obstacles such as waterfalls by leaping up to 11 feet high.

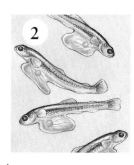

△ **1** The female salmon makes a small hole in the gravel on the riverbed and lays her eggs. The male then fertilizes them. **2** At birth, young salmon have a pouch on their sides that contains food.

▽ **3** After a year the young salmon develop red stripes on their sides. **4** By the time they are 6 inches long, the salmon are silver colored. They are now ready to journey down the river to the sea, where they will grow into adults and repeat the cycle.

Find out more
Fish
Migration
Reproduction

Satellites

A satellite is an object in space that travels around another object, such as a planet. This is called being in orbit. The Moon is a natural satellite that has orbited the Earth for billions of years. The other satellites orbiting the Earth are made by people. They are launched into orbit by space rockets. Some watch and measure the weather, some are used for communications, and some investigate outer space.

Communications satellites can carry telephone messages through space to the other side of the world. A message is beamed up from Earth to the satellite and then back down again to a receiver, which can be thousands of miles away from the caller.

▽ This satellite looks for cosmic rays. Its solar panels turn sunlight into electricity that the satellite needs to work. Its antenna sends information back to Earth. It also has thrusters, like tiny rockets, that turn the satellite to point in different directions.

radiation detector

antenna

solar panels

signals

◁ The Hubble space telescope is a satellite that takes pictures of objects far out in space and sends them back to Earth. This picture shows the space shuttle (and reuseable space rocket) putting the telescope into orbit high above the Earth.

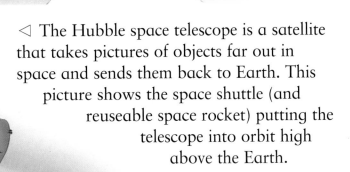

Find out more
Radio
Solar System
Space
exploration
Telephones
Universe
Weather

Science

Science is a study of the world around us. There are many kinds of sciences. Biology is a study of living things, geology is a study of the Earth, and astronomy is a study of stars and planets. Scientists look at things and try to explain what they see. They set up experiments to test their ideas.

leaf under microscope

△ A microscope makes things look much larger. Scientists use all sorts of tools to help them understand the world around us.

sinks   floats

◁ You can be a scientist too. These children are doing an experiment. First they guess which objects might float and which will sink. They sort them into piles.

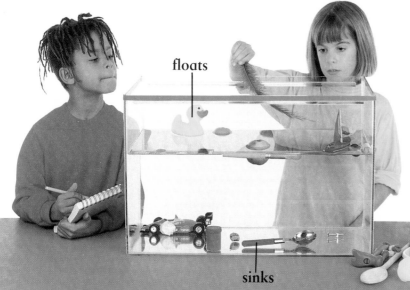

floats

sinks

◁ They drop the things from each pile into a tank of water to see if their guess was right. They think of reasons why some objects float and others sink. Do you know the reasons why?

Find out more
Biology
Chemistry
Physics

Scorpion

Scorpions are part of the same group of animals as spiders—the arachnids. They have eight legs, two powerful claws, and a stinging tail. Scorpions hide by day and only come out at night.

stinging tail

claw

Fact box

• The hairs on the scorpion's legs detect vibrations and help it find its prey.
• The imperial scorpion is up to 8 inches long.
• There are over 1,300 different species, found all over the world.

▷ Scorpions catch their prey in their claws and use the sting in their tail to kill it. The sting is also used in defense against predators like mongooses. Most scorpion stings are similar to those of a wasp, but some are strong enough to kill humans.

▽ Female scorpions keep their eggs inside their bodies until they are ready to hatch. When the young scorpions are born, they climb onto their mother's back.

△ Male scorpions may fight over a mate, wrestling with their claws and trying to sting each other. Before mating, the male and female also grapple in a complicated dance.

Find out more

Spider

Seabird

Some birds spend their whole lives near the sea, eating fish and nesting on cliffs or beaches. These birds are well adapted to life near the ocean: they usually have webbed feet for swimming, a sharp bill for catching fish, and waterproof feathers.

◁ **1** Seabirds need waterproof feathers so they don't get soggy and sink. Squirt water at a seabird feather and you will see how the natural oils on the feather repel the water.

△ Gannets are large, white seabirds with black-tipped wings. They fly above the surface of the water until they spot a school of fish. Then they dive deep into the ocean.

▷ **2** Take an even closer look at the feather with a magnifying glass. Can you see how the barbs link together? This flat surface is called the vane.

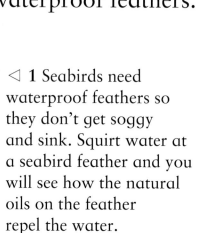

◁ Some seabirds, such as gulls and skuas, always stay near the shore. Others, like albatrosses and petrels, roam far out to sea. But all seabirds must return to land to nest. Guillemot eggs (left) have pointed ends, so they will roll in a circle instead of falling off the cliff.

Find out more
Albatross
Bird
Fish
Gull
Pelican
Penguin

Sea cow

The dugong and the manatee are sea cows. They are mammals that live in warm tropical seas, feeding on sea grass and water plants. The dugong is found in the Indian and Pacific oceans. The manatee lives in the tropical waters of the Americas, the West Indies, and Africa.

△ The dugong has a V-shaped tail. Adults grow to be 11 feet long. Unlike the manatee, male dugongs grow two tusklike teeth.

Fact box

• Female sea cows give birth to one baby at a time.
• Sea cows nurse their babies on nipples on their chest. They can hold the baby to a nipple with a flipper.
•Amazonian manatees gather in groups of 500.

▽ Manatees have round tails, shaped like paddles. They swim slowly and have bad eyesight.

△ Sea cows may live alone or in small groups. They seem to be affectionate animals— manatees often greet each other by touching noses, which looks as if they are kissing.

△ In the 1700s, sailors used to kill manatees for food. Manatees are now a protected species, but they are sometimes injured by boat propellers while swimming in shallow water.

Find out more
Dolphin
Seal and Sea lion
Walrus

Seahorse

Seahorses are fish that live in warm seas. Because they swim upright and are covered by bony armor, they do not look like fish. However, they are related to the stickleback.

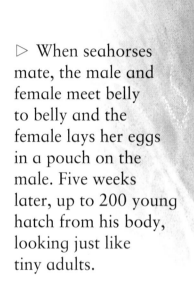

▷ When seahorses mate, the male and female meet belly to belly and the female lays her eggs in a pouch on the male. Five weeks later, up to 200 young hatch from his body, looking just like tiny adults.

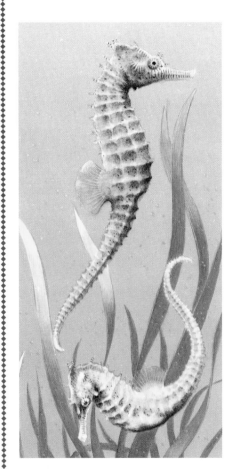

△ Seahorses spend much of their lives anchored by their tails to seaweed. They feed on shrimp and plankton, which they suck into their long mouths.

◁ The sea dragon is a type of seahorse found around the coasts of Australia. It is 5 feet long and is camouflaged by leafy-looking growths all over its body.

Find out more
Camouflage
Coral reef
Fish
Reproduction

Seal and Sea lion

Seals and sea lions are good swimmers and divers. They are mammals, so they have to come up to breathe, but they can stay underwater for up to 30 minutes. They feed on fish and penguins.

▽ While sea lions can walk on their flippers, seals cannot. Male sea lions have thick fur on their necks that looks like the mane of a lion.

▽ Seals catch their prey underwater, then they come to the surface to eat it.

◁ Female seals and sea lions feed their babies on milk that is extremely nourishing. The milk is full of fat and helps the babies grow quickly.

▽ Male elephant seals are the largest seals in the world. They get their name from their floppy noses, which look like trunks.

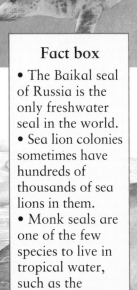

Fact box

• The Baikal seal of Russia is the only freshwater seal in the world.
• Sea lion colonies sometimes have hundreds of thousands of sea lions in them.
• Monk seals are one of the few species to live in tropical water, such as the Caribbean Sea.

Find out more

Dolphin
Killer whale
Penguin

Seashore

The seashore is where the land meets the sea. Some seashores are sandy, others may be rocky, muddy, or pebbly. Many different animals and plants live there. The seashore changes its shape all the time. This is because the waves pound against the beaches and rocks, slowly wearing them away.

△ Many seabirds live on the cliffs at the seaside. Puffins and gannets nest near the top, and murres lay their eggs on bare rock.

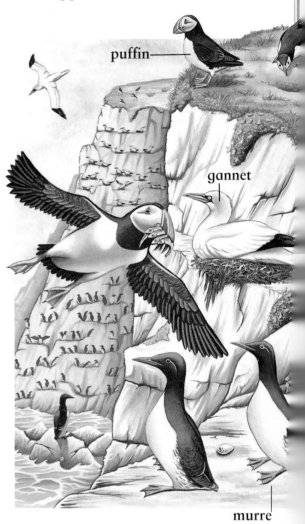

puffin

gannet

murre

△ Twice a day the sea comes far up the shore. This is called high tide.

△ The sea also goes out again twice every day. This is called low tide.

◁ Sand is made up of very tiny pieces of broken rock and shell. The color of sand depends on the color of the rock it is made of.

Always use a sun block and cover yourself to protect against the sun's harmful rays.

Find out more
Animals
Birds
Caves
Europe
Fossils
Oceans and seas

Seasons

Most of the world has four seasons. These are spring, summer, fall, and winter. This is because the Earth is tilted. As the Earth goes around the Sun, one half of the world leans closer to the Sun. This means that half of the Earth is warmer.

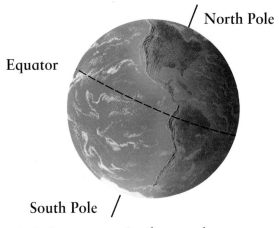

North Pole

Equator

South Pole

△ It is summer in the southern part of the world when it faces the Sun. In the northern part it is winter.

◁ Spring follows winter. The days become longer and warmer. Plants begin to grow and many animals have babies.

◁ Summer is the warmest season. Flowers bloom and fruits grow in the sunshine. It does not get dark until late.

◁ In the fall the days get shorter. The weather turns cooler. Trees may lose their leaves. Some birds fly to warmer places.

◁ Winter is the coldest season. It gets dark early in the evening. Plants stop growing and many trees are bare.

△ It is always hot near the equator. Often there is a dry season and a rainy season.

Find out more

Antarctica and the Arctic

Birds

Plants

Trees

Weather

Senses

How do you know what is happening around you, or what something feels like, or smells like? The answer is that you use your senses. Humans have five senses. These are sight, hearing, touch, taste, and smell. We often use more than one sense at a time. For example, when you eat something, you smell and taste it at the same time—and see it, too.

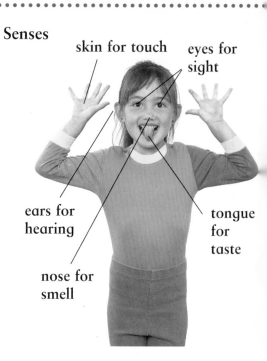

Senses

skin for touch

eyes for sight

ears for hearing

nose for smell

tongue for taste

▷ **1** Get a friend to guess what something is just by using his or her sense of touch. Cut a hole in the side of a large cardboard box. Make it big enough to put an arm through. Find a few different objects to put in the box.

△ Your sense organs pick up tastes, touches, smells, sounds, and sights. They send messages about these along your nerves to your brain. Your brain sorts out these messages and tells you what is going on around you.

Fact box

• Not everyone's senses work in the same way. For example, there are people who cannot easily tell red and green colors apart. This is because the light-sensitive cells in their eyes do not work properly.

△ **2** Do not let your friend see what the objects are. Can your friend tell what each one is just by feeling it through the hole?

△ Can you see the line of dots along the side of this fish? They act like another pair of eyes and detect movements made by other creatures nearby in the water. This helps the fish to find food and to escape from enemies.

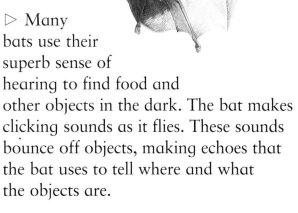

▷ Many bats use their superb sense of hearing to find food and other objects in the dark. The bat makes clicking sounds as it flies. These sounds bounce off objects, making echoes that the bat uses to tell where and what the objects are.

▽ One boy bursts a balloon, and the other boy points to where the sound is coming from. He hears the sound more loudly in one ear than the other. This tells him where the sound is being made.

△ Dogs have a much better sense of smell than humans. This dog has been trained to use its sense of smell to search for explosives.

△ This person's sense of sight does not work properly, so her guide dog helps her to find her way around.

Find out more
Color
Human body
Light and Lenses
Sound

Shark

Sharks are the most fearsome predators in the ocean. They are excellent hunters and find their prey either by its smell, or by tracking the tiny electrical currents that the prey's body gives out.

great white shark

hammerhead shark

△ The world's most dangerous shark is the great white. It can grow to be 40 feet long, and has a huge mouth full of sharp, pointed teeth. Great whites are found in warm waters all over the world. They sometimes attack bathers and surfers, but seals and sea lions are their favorite prey.

◁ The hammerhead shark uses its huge head to steer itself. Sharks are a kind of fish, but instead of fish scales they have rough skin, and instead of bone their skeleton is made of rubbery cartilage.

◁ At over 49 feet long, the whale shark is the largest of all fish. It eats some of the smallest creatures in the sea—plankton.

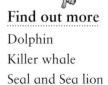

Find out more
Dolphin
Killer whale
Seal and Sea lion

Shellfish

Shellfish are water creatures whose soft bodies are protected by hard shells. Like slugs, snails, and octopuses, they are mollusks. They are found in fresh water and salt water all over the world.

△ When shellfish die, all that remains is the shell. If you go to the beach, collect as many different shells as you can. Later, you can display them on a board with their names underneath them.

Fact box

• Some shellfish have just one shell, others have a pair.
• Shells are made of minerals. These make the shells very hard.
• Shellfish have existed on Earth for 600 million years.

◁ Most shellfish feed by filtering tiny food particles from the water. Some shellfish stay on the same rock all their lives. They anchor themselves with a single sucker foot, or by threads.

▽ Mussels have two matching shells that clamp shut when they are in danger. They hold on to rocks using threads that are so strong they can resist huge storm waves.

lambis shell

top shell

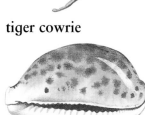

tiger cowrie

Find out more
Crab

Octopus and Squid

Ships and Boats

Boats have been used for thousands of years to carry people and goods across water. The first boats were rafts, made from logs or reeds tied together. Boats use sails, oars, or engines to push them through the water. Large, seagoing boats are called ships. There are many different kinds of ships and boats.

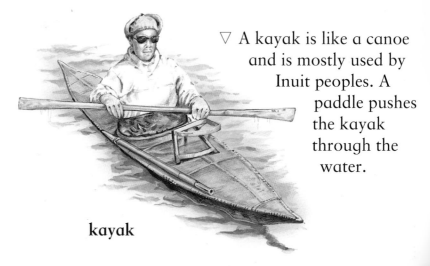

△ Long ago, the people of Polynesia explored the Pacific Ocean in boats like large canoes. They were searching for new islands.

▷ Huge passenger ships are called ocean liners or cruise ships. They are like floating hotels. The parts of a ship all have names. The front is called the bow and the back is called the stern.

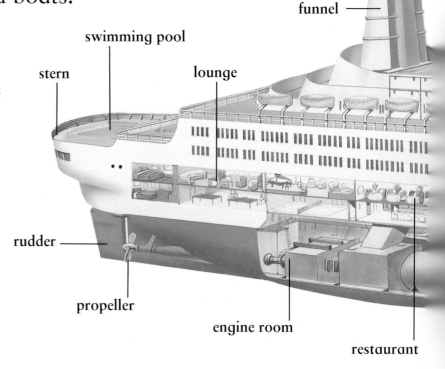

funnel

swimming pool

stern

lounge

rudder

propeller

engine room

restaurant

Viking longship

△ The Vikings were great sailors. They built strong, wooden ships, called longboats, which had square sails. They could also row their ships through the water with oars.

▽ A kayak is like a canoe and is mostly used by Inuit peoples. A paddle pushes the kayak through the water.

kayak

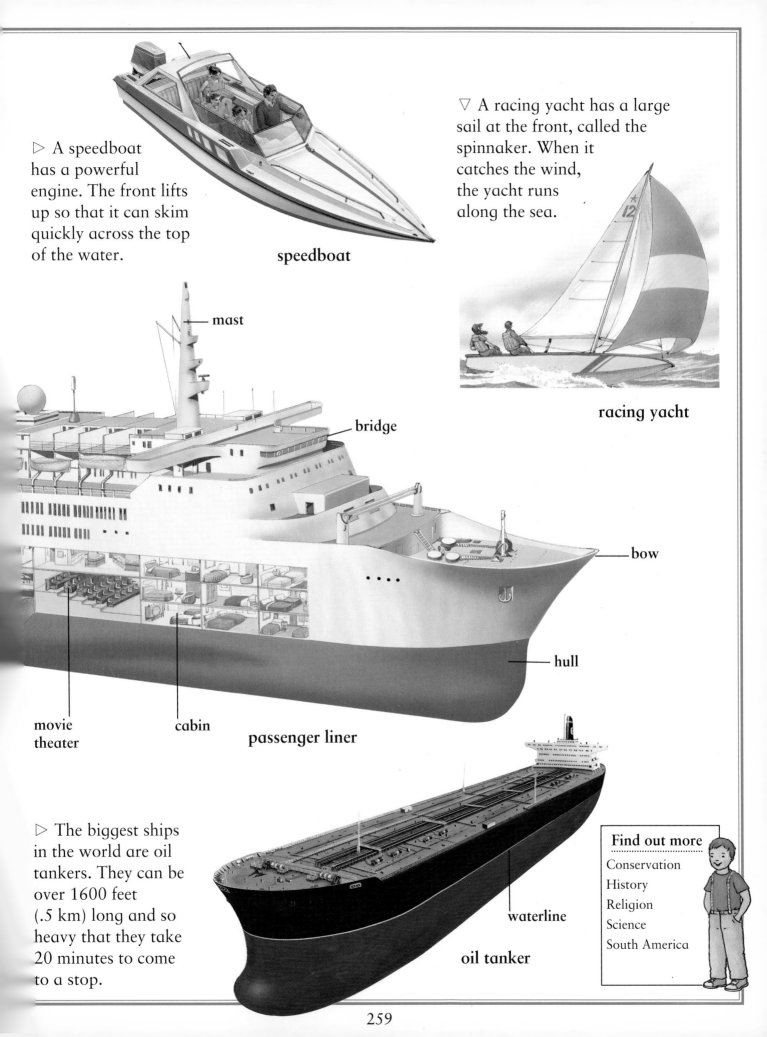

▷ A speedboat has a powerful engine. The front lifts up so that it can skim quickly across the top of the water.

speedboat

▽ A racing yacht has a large sail at the front, called the spinnaker. When it catches the wind, the yacht runs along the sea.

racing yacht

mast

bridge

bow

hull

movie theater

cabin

passenger liner

waterline

▷ The biggest ships in the world are oil tankers. They can be over 1600 feet (.5 km) long and so heavy that they take 20 minutes to come to a stop.

oil tanker

Find out more
Conservation
History
Religion
Science
South America

Shrimp and Prawn

Shrimp and prawns live in oceans, rivers, and lakes almost everywhere. They are related to lobsters but are smaller and are better swimmers. Prawns are slightly bigger than shrimp.

△ The pistol shrimp, which grows to about an inch and a half long, has very large claws. It snaps them together to stun its prey.

▽ **1** Make an underwater viewer to look at shrimp and prawns in rock pools. Get an adult to cut the bottom off a clear plastic bottle. Stretch plastic wrap over the cut end and secure with a rubber band.

▽ **2** You will need to keep still—these animals are easily frightened.

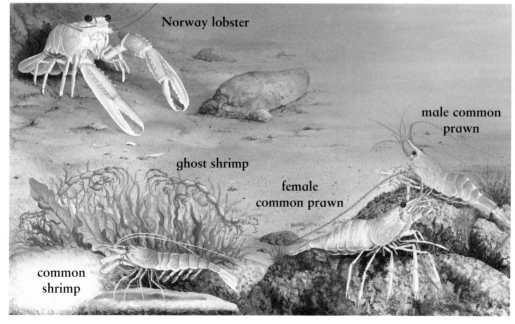

Norway lobster

ghost shrimp

male common prawn

female common prawn

common shrimp

◁ Shrimp and prawns often search for food on the seabed. They eat small plants and animals. They swim by flicking their fanlike tails.

Find out more
Crab
Shellfish

Skunk

Skunks live in woods and grassland in North and South America. They have long, furry tails and black-and-white fur. They are known for the foul smell they give off in defense.

△ Skunks are about the size of domestic cats, and weigh up to 7 pounds. They rest in their burrows by day, and come out at night to find plants, birds' eggs, insects, and small mammals to eat.

△ Skunks have around three babies in the spring. The young are born blind and do not leave the burrow for six weeks. When full-grown, they leave to find their own home.

▽ The skunk has a special way of dealing with a predator such as a lynx. First it thumps its paws on the ground. Then it turns around, flinging up its rear legs to expose its bottom.

Fact box

• The most common skunk in North America is the striped skunk.
• The other two types are the hog-nosed skunk and the spotted skunk.
• Skunks can spray an attacker from a distance of 13 feet. The smell lasts for days.

▷ If the attacker does not heed the warning, the skunk lowers its legs and squirts a jet of liquid from glands near the tail. The smell is so awful that few predators return for more.

Find out more
Badger
Otter

Sloth

Someone who is lazy or slow might be described as being slothful. Looking at the sloth, it is easy to see why. The sloth spends its life hanging in the trees by its hooked claws, and it hardly ever moves at all.

Fact box
• Sloths are found in the rain forests of South America.
• Once every two to three weeks, they climb down to the ground to go to the bathroom.
• Sloths can fall asleep in their hanging position.

▽ The female gives birth to one young, which she carries on her stomach for about five weeks after its birth. The baby sloth stays on by clinging to its mother's fur.

△ Sloths wake at night to feed on leaves and fruit. The hair on their coats hangs down from the belly to the back so the rainwater can flow off easily. Some species have algae growing in their coats. This gives them a greenish color that camouflages them in the trees.

△ Although sloths move slowly on land, they can swim well. They are not afraid to cross large rivers and swamps to find food and new trees to live in.

Find out more
Camouflage
Mammal
Monkey

Slug and Snail

Slugs and snails are found all over the world, both on land and in water. They have feelers on their heads, soft bodies, and a single muscular foot that is also their stomach. Snails have shells, but slugs do not.

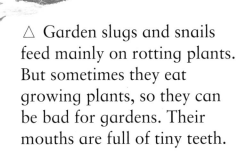

◁ Watch how slugs and snails move by placing them on a piece of clear glass or plastic. You will see that they ooze a trail of slime to ease their way along.

△ Garden slugs and snails feed mainly on rotting plants. But sometimes they eat growing plants, so they can be bad for gardens. Their mouths are full of tiny teeth.

▽ Snails are known for moving slowly, but a snail race can still be very exciting. On a board, make three lanes with string held in place by tacks. Chalk a line at the start and at the finish, then start them off. The first one past the finish line is the winner.

Fact box

• Land species have lungs to breathe; water species have gills.
• The giant land snail can be 12 inches long.
• Tropical cone snails feed on fish. First they paralyze them by injecting nerve poison from a tooth on the end of their tongue.

Find out more
Centipede
Fish
Habitat
Shellfish

Solar System

The Solar System is made up of the Sun and the nine planets that orbit (travel around) it. One of these planets is the Earth. Some of these planets have moons orbiting around them. Comets and asteroids travel around the Solar System, too. As far as we know, the Earth is the only place in the Solar System where anything lives.

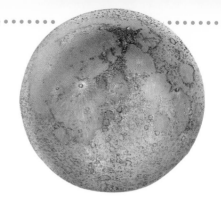

△ The Earth has one moon. It is nearly 240,000 miles from Earth. Its diameter is only a quarter of the Earth's.

 Never look straight at the Sun, either with binoculars or just with your eyes.

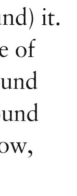

◁ Try looking at the Moon through a pair of binoculars. Can you see the craters on the surface?

The Solar System is enormous. If the Sun was only the size of a football, the Earth would be the size of a pinhead, 80 feet away. Pluto would be about a mile from the Sun.

▷ Jupiter and Saturn are huge. They are made of gas and liquid. Jupiter is the biggest of all the planets. The others could all fit inside it easily.

▽ Mercury, Venus, Earth, and Mars are small, rocky planets. Mercury is nearest to the Sun.

Jupiter

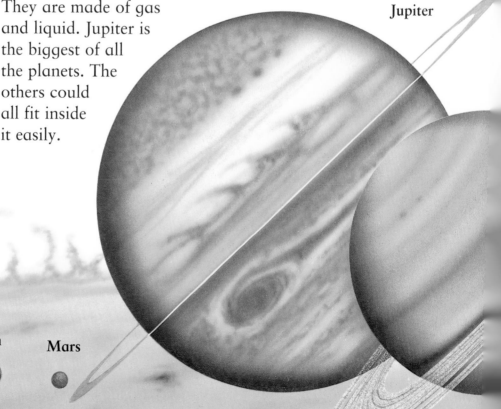

Mercury

Venus

Earth

Mars

▽ This is the spacecraft Voyager 2. It is a space probe. It was sent from Earth in 1977 to explore outer space. It reached Neptune in 1989. Scientists have learned a lot about planets from Voyager 2 and other spacecraft like it.

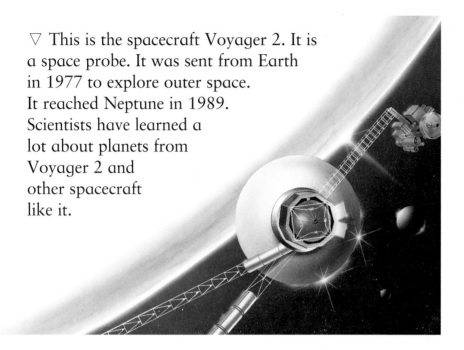

Fact box
• The Earth takes 365 days to orbit the Sun. This is one Earth year. Planets farther from the Sun take longer, so they have longer years. Pluto's is the longest at 248 Earth years. A Mercury year is only 88 days long.

▷ If you are lucky, you might see streaks of light, called shooting stars or meteors, in the night sky. They are made by rocks called meteors hurtling into the Earth's atmosphere and burning up.

Saturn

◁ Some planets have rings of solid material around them. Jupiter and Neptune have rings of dust. Uranus has rings of rocks. Saturn has the most rings. They are made up of millions of lumps of ice.

▽ Pluto is the farthest planet from the Sun. It is smaller than the Earth's moon.

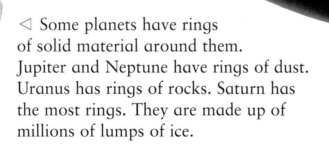

Uranus

Neptune

Find out more
Earth
Satellites
Space exploration
Universe

• **Pluto**

Solids

A solid is one of the three states of matter. The others are liquids and gases. A solid has a fixed shape. It does not flow around like a liquid or a gas. This is because the atoms are joined firmly together, and can hardly move around at all.

△ In some solids, the atoms are arranged in neat rows. This sort of solid is called a crystal.

◁ **1** This is how to make sugar crystals grow. Stir some sugar into warm water until no more will dissolve.

▷ **2** Pour the liquid into a saucer and leave it in a warm place, so that the water evaporates. Can you see the crystals beginning to form?

△ These objects are made from solids that are not crystals. Although their atoms are not in neat rows, they still cannot move around.

▽ Some solids are softer than others. The soft, gray substance in pencils is called graphite. It rubs easily onto the paper when you write.

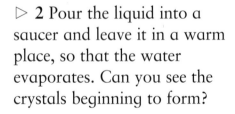

△ Diamond and graphite are both made of carbon, but their atoms are arranged in a different way. Diamond is extremely hard. It is used in jewelry and to make tools for cutting, such as drills.

Find out more

Gases

Materials

Sound

Sound is made by vibrations. When you speak, you make vibrations in the air. These vibrations spread out. Anyone whose ears can pick up the vibrations will hear the sound of your voice. Sound can travel through solids and liquids as well as through air and other gases.

▽ To see the vibrations that give us sound, cover a plastic pot with a piece of balloon, and secure it with a rubber band. Sprinkle salt on it. Speak near the balloon. The vibrations will make the salt grains jump up and down.

Loudness

rocket on takeoff 150–190 decibels

◁ The loudness of a sound depends on the size of the vibrations it makes. Sounds are loud when the vibrations are very big, and soft when they are small. Loudness is measured in units called decibels. The noise of a road drill is over 100 decibels.

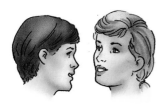

motorcycle 70–90 decibels

talking quietly 30–60 decibels

△ This road drill makes a very loud noise. Sounds this loud can damage people's ears. The workers using the drill must cover their ears to protect them.

▽ As sound spreads, the molecules making up the air are squashed together, pulled apart, squashed again, and so on, making sound waves.

leaves rustling 20 decibels

A sound can be high-pitched or low-pitched. The pitch of a sound (how high it is) depends on its frequency (the number of vibrations it makes per second).

▷ Try this experiment to make high- and low-pitched sounds. Pour some water into jars, so that the level is different in each. Tap the jars with a pen. Which jar makes the sound with the highest pitch?

▷ Sonar is a way of finding things under water, using sound. A sonar machine on a ship sends "blip" sounds into the water. When these hit an object, they bounce back as echoes. The farther away the object is, the longer the echo takes to return to the control ship.

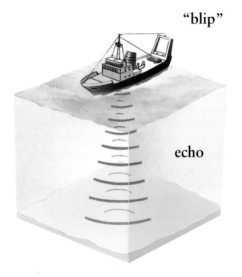

"blip"

echo

Fact box

• A rocket taking off makes a sound a million times louder than a clap of thunder.
• Some animals can hear sounds that are too high- or low-pitched for human beings to hear.

◁ Some dolphins make clicking sounds and then listen for their echoes. This helps them to find their way around in murky water. It works in a similar way to sonar. Some kinds of whales communicate with each other using sound. The noises they make can travel hundreds of miles across the oceans.

▷ This brass horn looks like a long, coiled tube with a funnel. It makes a sound when the musician blows into the tube and the air inside it vibrates. The funnel spreads the sound out so you can hear it. Do you know any other brass instruments?

△ The cello is a stringed instrument. It makes a sound when the strings vibrate from side to side. This happens when a musician draws a bow across the strings or plucks them. Guitars and violins are also stringed instruments.

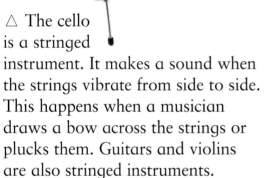

△ This girl is playing a flute. The boy is playing a whistle. Both of these are wind instruments. Like brass instruments, these make a sound when the musician blows into them and the air in the tube vibrates.

◁ This girl is playing an electronic keyboard. Keyboards like these are sometimes called synthesizers. A synthesizer makes sounds through a loudspeaker. Each key makes a note of a different pitch.

Find out more
Energy
Physics
Senses

South America

South America is the fourth largest continent. It has hot and cold deserts and large grassy plains. Down one side runs a long line of mountains called the Andes. The world's largest rain forest grows around the Amazon River. Many people in South America live in crowded cities and are very poor.

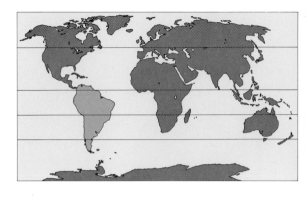

△ South America is shown in purple. It is joined to North America by a thin stretch of land, called Central America.

▷ The people who live around Lake Titicaca, high up in the Andes Mountains, build their boats and houses out of reeds.

◁ Statues and ruins are all that is left of the ancient cities of South America. This statue is from a city called Tiahuanaco (tee-ah-**wa**-nih-**ko**).

▷ People raise llamas for their meat and wool. Llamas also carry heavy goods.

270

▷ Cowboys, called gauchos, look after enormous herds of cattle on the grassy plains of Argentina. These grasslands are called the pampas.

▽ Angel Falls, in the rain forest of Venezuela, is the highest waterfall in the world.

▷ Macaws live in the lush Amazon rain forest. Snakes, monkeys, and big cats also live there.

scarlet macaw

◁ Rio de Janeiro is the main port of Brazil. A huge statue of Christ, on Corcovado Mountain, stands high above Rio's beautiful bay.

Find out more
Conservation
Grasslands
World

Space exploration

To find out more about the planets and stars, scientists send rockets carrying people and objects into space. People who travel into space are called astronauts. They wear special suits in space to survive. Machines that can travel into space are called spacecraft. One of the best known is the Space Shuttle.

▽ The Space Shuttle can carry up to seven astronauts into space. Its doors open up in space to release its cargo of scientific instruments. An astronaut controls a robot arm to move the cargo.

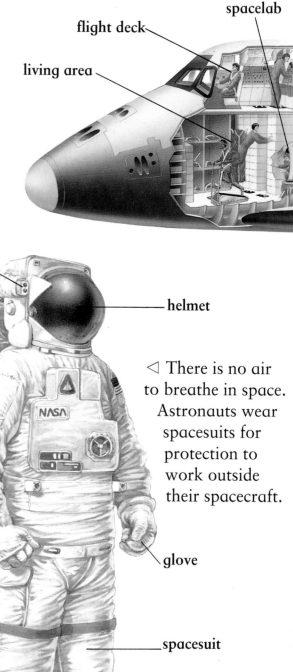

tunnel to spacelab

flight deck

living area

Saturn V

radio

air supply

helmet

◁ There is no air to breathe in space. Astronauts wear spacesuits for protection to work outside their spacecraft.

◁ The biggest rocket ever built was called the Saturn V. It carried the first astronauts to the Moon in 1969.

glove

spacesuit

boot

Space Shuttle

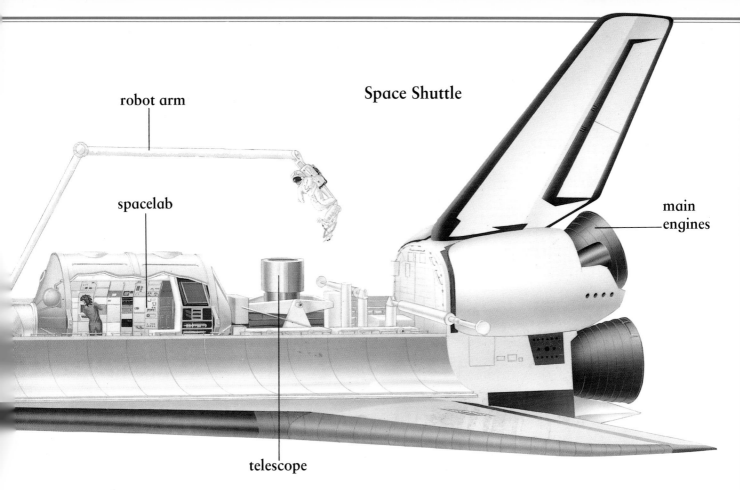

robot arm

spacelab

telescope

main engines

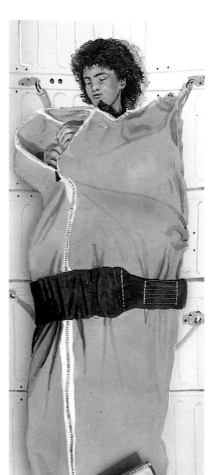

◁ The Space Shuttle takes off with a huge fuel tank and two booster rockets to blast it into space. It takes only a few minutes for it to reach space.

booster rocket

◁ In space nothing has any weight. Astronauts have to move around carefully. They are strapped into their sleeping bags to stop them from floating around.

Satellites and probes

Rockets also carry satellites and probes into space. These machines send back information to Earth.

Meteosat

▷ The giant Hubble Space Telescope sends back pictures of stars and galaxies to astronomers on Earth.

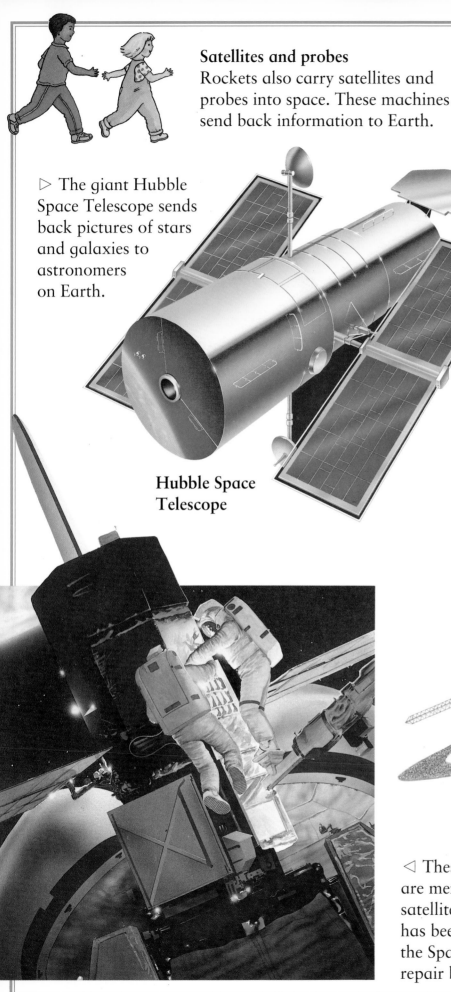

Hubble Space Telescope

△ Meteosat watches weather patterns. It sends information to computers on Earth.

▽ Voyager 2 was a probe that traveled out to the planets. It sent back pictures of Jupiter, Saturn, Uranus, and Neptune.

Voyager 2

◁ These astronauts are mending a broken satellite. The satellite has been taken into the Space Shuttle's repair bay.

Find out more
Inventions
Moon
Universe

Spider

Spiders belong to the class of animals called arachnids. They feed mainly on insects. Most spiders have large, hairy, round abdomens (rear body parts) and eight legs. All spiders make silk, and many spin webs.

◁ The female black widow spider is one of the few spiders with venom (poison) harmful to humans. Most people bitten by it do recover fully.

Fact box

• The goliath bird-eating spider is the biggest spider in the world. It is large enough to cover a dinner plate.
• Tropical orb-web spiders build some of the largest webs—nearly 7 feet across.

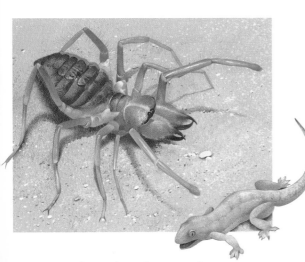

△ Camel spiders live in deserts in Africa and Asia. They do not spin webs, but pounce on their prey and crush them in their strong jaws. They feed on scorpions, birds, and small lizards.

▷ Many spiders spin webs of sticky silk to catch their prey. Silk is very strong and it also stretches. Here a garden spider wraps a fly in its silk, then stuns it with venom from its fangs.

◁ Spiders live in many places, from hot deserts to mountains and lakes. Some spiders that live near water eat small fish.

Find out more
Fly
Insect
Scorpion

Sports

People play sports for many reasons. It may be their job or they may just do it for fun. Being active helps them to stay fit and healthy. Some sports are played by one person. Others are played by two or more people. In many sports two teams compete with each other. Some sports, like horse racing, involve animals as well as people.

△ Soccer is played all over the world. In some countries it is called football. Players need great skill to control the ball with their feet.

▷ Baseball can be played at all ages. This young pitcher is developing his skills in Little League games.

◁ Gymnasts start learning when they are very young. They practice how to perform exercises on the floor and on special pieces of equipment, like this one, called the bar.

◁ In Mongolia, boys and girls as young as five dress up to take part in horse races.

▷ Ice hockey is one of the most popular North American sports. It is a fast and tough game. Players wear helmets and pads for protection.

△ Swimmers train hard to swim well and fast. They learn different strokes, called the breaststroke, backstroke, crawl, and butterfly.

▽ When two people play tennis against each other it is called singles. When four play it is called doubles.

▷ The Olympic Games are held every four years. Countries send their best athletes to compete.

Find out more

Cars
Clothes
Health
Human body
Mountains
Oceans and seas

Squirrel

Most squirrels have big, bushy tails and live in trees. They are active during the day, running from branch to branch in search of nuts, fruit, and seeds.

▷ The red squirrel, like the one seen here, is smaller than its gray cousin. In Britain, red squirrels are being forced from their woodland homes by the more aggressive gray squirrels, which were imported from North America about 100 years ago.

▽ The prairie dog is a burrowing squirrel that lives on North American grasslands. Their large underground burrows, called towns, contain up to 1,000 prairie dogs.

◁ Squirrels love seeds like acorns, which they gnaw with their sharp front teeth. In the fall, they sometimes bury a supply in the ground to last them through the winter.

Find out more
Habitat
Mammal
Mouse
Rat
Reproduction

Starfish

Starfish are found on ocean floors worldwide, especially in the warm waters of the Indian and Pacific oceans. Though starfish are star-shaped, they are not fish. They have no head and no brain; all they have is five or more arms, a central body, and a mouth.

1
2
3
4

◁ A starfish has hundreds of strong suckers called tube feet. If it is turned upside down it uses these tube feet to turn over again. **1** It curls the tips of its arms around to grip the rocks with its suckers. **2** When it has a hold, it pulls itself over slowly. **3, 4** It flops down the right way up, and moves off.

△ There are 1,500 species of starfish in the world's oceans. Many are brightly colored.

▷ Some kinds of starfish have lots of legs, like this sunstar. If a starfish loses a leg, it can easily grow another.

▽ Starfish eat shellfish. To eat a mussel, the starfish opens the shell with its powerful suckers, then pushes its stomach out of its mouth and onto the body of the shellfish.

Fact box

• The crown-of-thorns starfish feeds on coral, and this can badly damage the reef.
• Starfish sense changes in light with the light-sensitive spots on the ends of their arms.
• Some starfish lay up to a million eggs in a year.

Find out more

Coral reef
Octopus and Squid
Shellfish
Shrimp and Prawn

Stories

Stories tell you about events. Some stories are about real things, others are made up. Long ago, people told each other stories about their gods or about real people who had done amazing things. Now we read stories in books and comics or watch them in movies and on television.

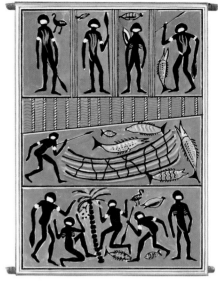

△ The Australian Aborigines paint stories of how they believe the land was made.

▽ Use your imagination to write your own story. Make it a scary, funny, or magical story. Draw pictures of the characters. Show what they did.

▷ The ancient Greeks told stories about a winged horse named Pegasus. He was caught by Bellerophon and did many brave deeds.

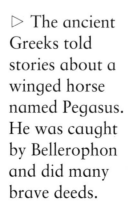

◁ In Africa, the Ashanti people, who live in Ghana, tell stories about a spider called Ananse who likes to play tricks.

▷ Comic strips tell stories with pictures. The words people say are written in speech bubbles.

▷ Jack and the Beanstalk is a folktale. Jack climbs a huge beanstalk to steal a magic hen from a wicked and cruel giant.

◁ The story of the Wizard of Oz was made into a famous film. Dorothy helps a scarecrow, a cowardly lion, and a tin man.

Find out more

Africa
Art and artists
Books
Dance
Drama

Sun

The Sun is a star. It is a dazzling ball of burning gases. The Sun is the nearest, most important star to the Earth. It gives us light and warmth. The Earth is almost 93 million miles (149.5 million km) from the Sun. If the Earth were closer it would burn up. If it were farther away it would be freezing cold.

△ During an eclipse the Moon hides the Sun. This is the only time that we can see the clouds of white gas, called the corona, that surround the Sun.

Never look straight at the Sun. It will damage your eyes.

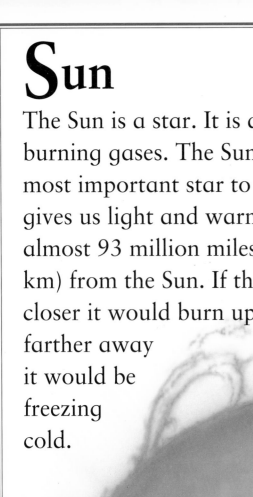

core

prominences are jets of hot gas

sunspots are the coolest parts of the Sun

Find out more

Earth
Energy
Light
Planets
Plants
Seashore
Seasons
Universe
Weather

> A telephone is linked to an exchange. Exchanges are connected to each other, by cables, radio, and sometimes by satellite links. All these things make up the telephone network.

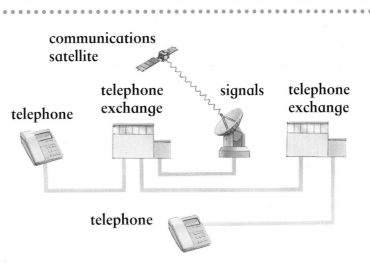

communications satellite

telephone

telephone exchange

signals

telephone exchange

telephone

△ The telephones that we use at home are linked to the local exchange by wires. Signals go along these as pulses of electricity. Some telephone cables are made of thin glass fibers called optical fibers. Signals travel along these as flashes of light.

△ A fax machine plugs into a telephone line, just like an ordinary telephone. It has a scanner that turns words and pictures into electrical signals. The fax sends these to another fax machine.

△ The other fax machine turns the signals back into words and pictures. It prints them onto paper.

the other person talks into a container

3

string must be pulled tight

◁ 3 Vibrations made by your voice travel along the string. They make the other pot vibrate. Your friend hears these vibrations as your voice.

Find out more
Electricity
Inventions
Satellites
Sound

Television

What sort of television programs do you like best? To make a televison program, a camera has to take pictures. These go from the camera to a television station, and on to a transmitter. This sends them to your television set, along wires or on radio waves. Satellite television programs travel on microwaves.

△ The pictures on these screens are from security cameras. A guard watches for intruders. A system like this is called closed circuit television.

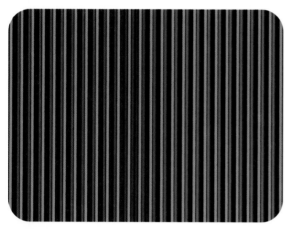

△ This is a magnified close-up of a television screen. You can see bands of red, green, and blue. All television pictures are made up of just these three colors.

△ This camera is recording a sports event. The camera operator sees the picture the camera is taking on a small television screen.

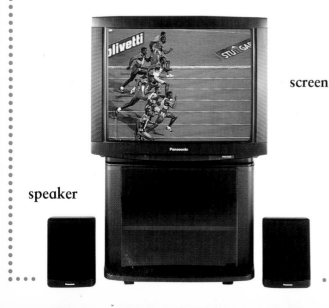

screen

speaker

◁ A television set turns signals from the television station into the pictures you see on the screen. It plays sound through the loudspeakers.

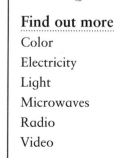

Find out more
Color
Electricity
Light
Microwaves
Radio
Video

288

Tiger

Tigers are the biggest of all cats. They live in the grasslands and forests of Asia, where their striped coat gives them good camouflage when they hunt.

△ Female tigers give birth to between one and three cubs. The cubs stay with their mother for over a year.

△ A tiger slowly stalks its prey, a deer, through the long grass. When it is close enough, it makes a sudden dash, leaps onto the deer's back, and knocks it down. A quick bite to the neck kills the deer.

◁ Tigers are hunted for their beautiful coats, and for their bones and body parts, which are used in traditional Chinese medicine. Because of this, tigers are nearly extinct.

Find out more
Cat (wild)
Cheetah
Lion

Time

We use clocks and watches to measure time exactly in hours, minutes, and seconds. In the ancient past, people measured time roughly in days, nights, and seasons. Later, people used shadow clocks, candle clocks, and sundials. At sea they used sand clocks such as the hourglass.

candle clock

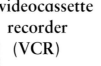

◁ Candle clocks were marked in sections. The candle burned away one section every hour. People could tell the time by the number of sections left.

videocassette recorder (VCR)

△ This videocassette recorder has a digital clock. It uses the clock to start a recording at the right time.

alarm clock

△ An alarm clock can be set to wake you up in time for something. Many children use alarm clocks to wake them up in time for school.

stopwatch

△ This boy uses a stopwatch to time his friend running a race. He stops the watch when his friend crosses over the finishing line.

Find out more
Earth
Machines
Moon
Seasons
Year

Trains

All over the world, trains pull heavy loads along rails. The rails make it easier for the wheels to turn. The first trains used steam engines to drive the wheels. Now, most trains run on electricity or diesel fuel. Trains carry people and goods for long distances, at high speeds.

steam train

△ Steam trains were invented 200 years ago. They used coal or wood to make steam to drive the wheels.

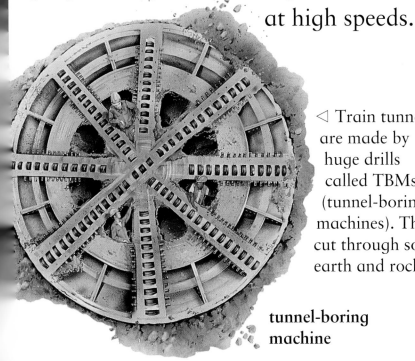

◁ Train tunnels are made by huge drills called TBMs (tunnel-boring machines). They cut through soft earth and rock.

tunnel-boring machine

△ Cities like New York, Boston, and San Francisco have train systems. They run under the city on electrically charged rails.

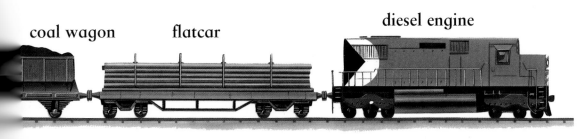

coal wagon   flatcar   diesel engine

◁ Trains that carry goods are called freight trains. Some can pull over 100 wagons.

TGV

◁ The world's fastest passenger train is the TGV in France. It can travel as fast as 186 miles (300 km) per hour.

Find out more
Electricity
Inventions
Machines

Trees

Trees are plants. They are among the largest living things on Earth. Many of them live for hundreds of years.

Trees give food and shelter to birds, insects, and many other animals. Mushrooms and other fungi grow on their roots and on dead tree stumps.

△ Each year, a layer of wood grows inside the trunk of a tree and makes a ring. You can tell the age of a tree by counting the number of rings in the trunk.

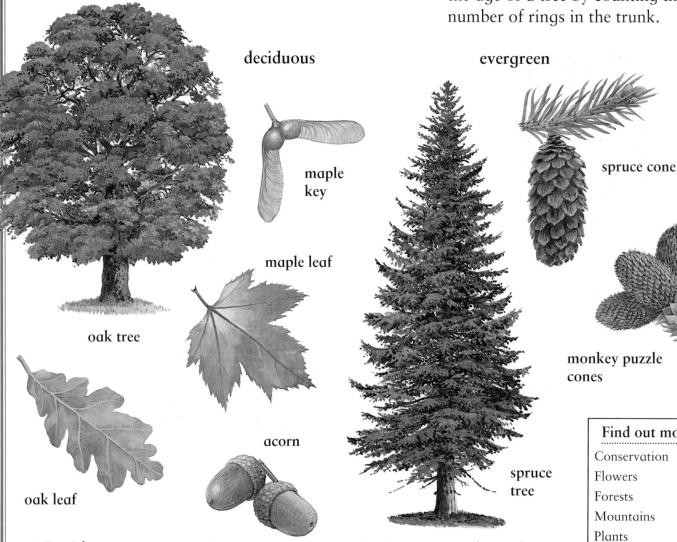

deciduous

evergreen

maple key

spruce cone

maple leaf

oak tree

monkey puzzle cones

oak leaf

acorn

spruce tree

△ Deciduous trees start to lose their leaves in the fall and have no leaves in winter. They grow new leaves in the spring.

△ Evergreen trees keep their leaves all year. Many have spiky, needlelike leaves that are not harmed by the cold.

Find out more

Conservation
Flowers
Forests
Mountains
Plants
Prehistoric life
Seasons

Trucks

Trucks are made to carry all kinds of things. They take food and other goods from farms and factories to stores. They carry all your furniture and possessions when you move house. They are built to be very strong and can travel long distances—even from one end of the country to the other.

△ This truck is called a road train. Road trains can pull three huge trailers. They are used in Australia.

△ The crane on the back of a logging truck is used to lift logs onto the trailer. This truck is used in places with large forests.

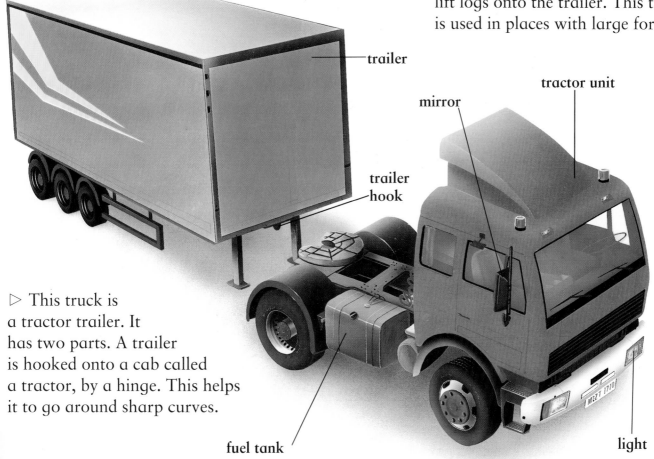

trailer

tractor unit

mirror

trailer hook

fuel tank

light

▷ This truck is a tractor trailer. It has two parts. A trailer is hooked onto a cab called a tractor, by a hinge. This helps it to go around sharp curves.

◁ Small pick-up trucks may have open backs. This is useful for short-distance transportation.

Find out more
Conservation
Machines
Roads

Turtle and Tortoise

Turtles and tortoises are reptiles that live in warm climates. Turtles are found in water; tortoises are slow land animals. The soft bodies of both animals are protected by a heavy shell.

△ Many turtles spend nearly all their lives in the sea. Their legs are shaped like paddles, which help them swim. Only females ever come onto land. They do this to lay eggs—on the same beach as they were born.

◁ Tortoises are found in Africa, Asia, Europe, and North and South America. They grow slowly and can live to be over 150 years old.

◁ **1** The female turtle crawls out of the sea to lay her eggs. **2** She buries them in a hole, then returns to the water. The sun's heat keeps them warm until they are ready to hatch.

▷ **3** Left on their own, the tiny babies must break free of their eggs and dig their way out of the hole. **4** They must hurry to the sea before they are eaten by other animals.

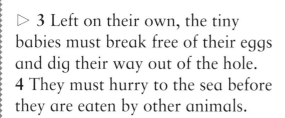

Find out more
Chameleon
Lizard
Reptile
Reproduction

Universe

The universe contains all light and energy, and all living things. It is very hard to imagine how big the universe really is. The Earth, the Sun, the other planets, and all the stars that you can see in the sky at night make up our galaxy, called the Milky Way. Some people talk about the Milky Way galaxy being the universe, but it is only one tiny part of the whole universe. There are many galaxies in the universe.

△ Even when you look through a telescope you can only see a tiny part of the universe.

◁ This picture is of huge groups of stars, called galaxies. It was taken in space by the Hubble Space Telescope.

Hubble Space Telescope

The life of a star

New stars are being made all the time. They shine for a very long time and then they die. A red giant is a huge, old star.

Little Dipper

Southern Cross

△ Long ago, people gave names to patterns made by stars in the sky. These patterns are called constellations. The Little Dipper can be seen by people living in the northern part of the world. The Southern Cross can be seen by people living in the southern part.

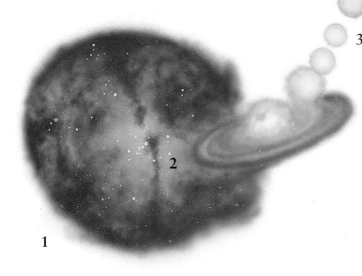

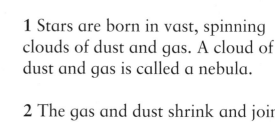

1 Stars are born in vast, spinning clouds of dust and gas. A cloud of dust and gas is called a nebula.

2 The gas and dust shrink and join to form lots of balls. These become a cluster of baby stars.

3 As a star gets hotter it begins to shine. Most stars, like our Sun, shine steadily nearly all their lives.

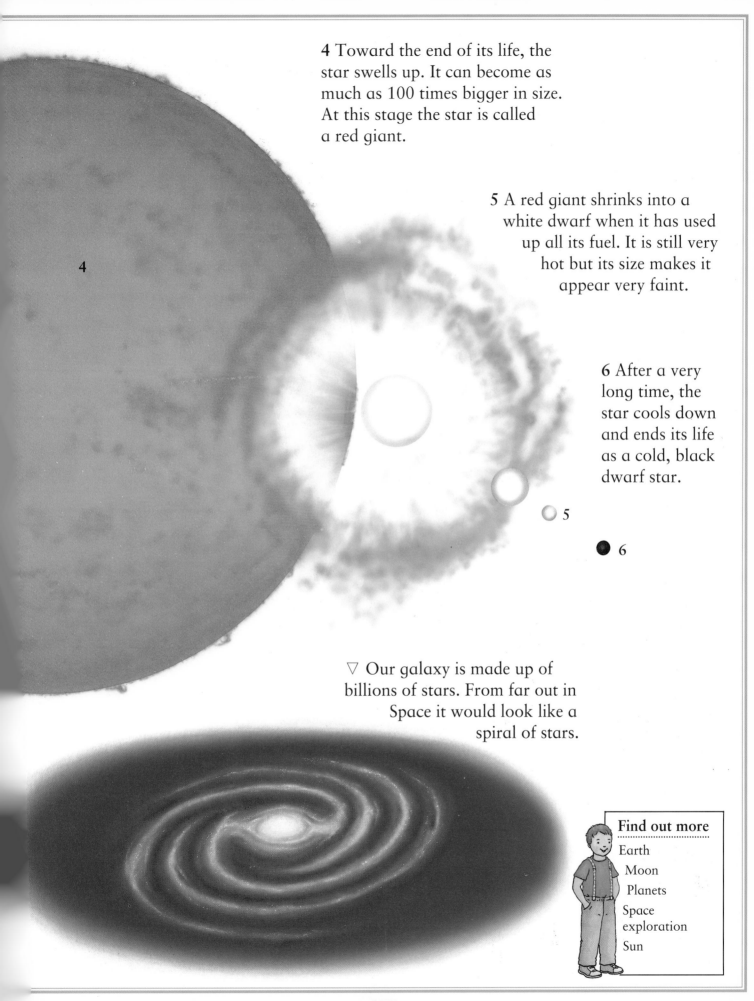

4 Toward the end of its life, the star swells up. It can become as much as 100 times bigger in size. At this stage the star is called a red giant.

4

5 A red giant shrinks into a white dwarf when it has used up all its fuel. It is still very hot but its size makes it appear very faint.

6 After a very long time, the star cools down and ends its life as a cold, black dwarf star.

5

6

▽ Our galaxy is made up of billions of stars. From far out in Space it would look like a spiral of stars.

Find out more

Earth

Moon

Planets

Space exploration

Sun

Video

Video is a way of recording moving pictures. The recording is done on videotape. This is like the tape used in a music cassette. With a video camera, you can record your own moving pictures and play them on television, using a videocassette recorder (VCR).

▽ A camcorder is a video camera and recorder all in one. You look through the viewfinder to see what you are recording.

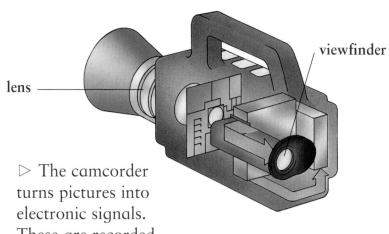

lens

viewfinder

▷ The camcorder turns pictures into electronic signals. These are recorded on the video tape.

◁ A VCR is used to record television programs for watching later. It can also play prerecorded video tapes, such as films and cartoons.

◁ The word video also describes moving pictures made by a computer. That's why computer games are sometimes called video games.

Find out more
Camera
Electricity
Recording
Television

Volcano

Under the Earth's hard crust lies hot, molten rock called magma. Sometimes pressure builds up under the Earth and pushes the magma up through cracks in the crust. This is how a volcano erupts. When it reaches the surface, the magma is known as lava. Some volcanoes erupt with a bang and shoot gas, dust, and lava into the air.

△ These huge fountains of hot water and steam are called geysers. They are often found near volcanoes. Water is heated by the hot rocks under the ground and gushes to the surface through cracks in the Earth's crust.

△ **1** Make a model volcano. Put about two teaspoons of bicarbonate of soda into a spice jar. Build a clay model of a volcano around the jar.

△ **2** Pour 3.5 fluid ounces of vinegar into the jar and watch your volcano erupt. To make colored lava, add food coloring to the vinegar.

▽ When a volcano erupts, molten rock flows along underground channels and then pours out of the top of the volcano. As the lava cools, it forms a cone-shaped mountain.

△ The hole at the top of a volcano is called the crater. In some volcanoes, smoke rises from the crater all the time.

Find out more
Earth
Energy
Fuels
Melting and Boiling

Vulture

Vultures are large, strange-looking birds with wide wingspans. They are found worldwide—on mountains and plains, and in forests. They feed on rotting meat.

◁ Many species of vulture, like the king vulture (left), have no head or neck feathers. This keeps them clean when feeding. The king vulture's brightly colored skin flaps are used in mating displays.

△ Many vulture species have incredible eyesight. They fly high in the air, looking for predators' kills.

▽ Vultures do a vital job because they clean up the carcasses left behind by predators. Once they spot a carcass, they glide down to feed. Some vultures have adapted to living in towns, and scavenge on garbage dumps.

△ Vultures, like this white-backed vulture, often sit in the trees around a lion or hyena kill, waiting until the larger animals have had their fill.

Eurasian griffin

Ruppell's griffin

African white-backed vulture

lappet-faced vulture

Find out more
Birds
Eagle
Owl

Water

All life on Earth needs water. Without it everything would die. Water covers nearly three-fourths of the world. There is salty water in the oceans and seas, and fresh water in lakes, rivers, and ponds. Frozen water, or ice, usually covers the oceans around Antarctica and in the Arctic. All these watery places are home to many different plants and animals.

pond skater

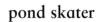

△ A pond skater can walk on water because of a force called surface tension. This force makes a thin stretchy layer on the water.

▷ When water is a liquid it flows and spreads. When it is poured into a container, it has a flat surface.

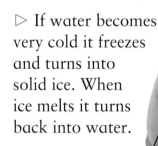

water

▷ If water becomes very cold it freezes and turns into solid ice. When ice melts it turns back into water.

ice

▽ When water is very hot it boils. Bubbles rise up, burst, and release steam.

steam

▽ When steam hits something cold, it cools and turns into water droplets. This change is called condensation.

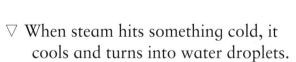

condensation

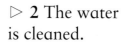

▷ **2** The water is cleaned.

How we use water
▷ **1** Water falls as rain and runs into rivers and streams. It is collected and stored in big lakes called reservoirs.

▽ **3** Water is pumped through pipes into houses.

△ **5** The water is cleaned. Then it flows back into a river or the sea.

△ **4** After it has been used, the water goes down through drainpipes into the sewers.

▽ Plants need water. Their roots soak up water from the soil. The water travels up the stems to the leaves where it helps to make food.

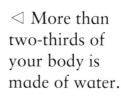

Fact box

• You lose water from your body when you sweat, breathe, and go to the toilet.

• You need to drink about one quart of water a day to stay healthy.

• You could not live for more than three days without water.

◁ More than two-thirds of your body is made of water.

◁ In the dry savannas of Africa, groups of animals gather at the water hole. As they take a long drink, they watch out for hungry lions.

▽ This mangrove swamp is a wet area of land near the sea. Mangrove trees have long, strong roots to anchor them in the mud.

◁ A salmon swims from the sea to lay its eggs in the river where it was born. Some bears wait near waterfalls to catch salmon.

▽ Many different plants grow in and around ponds. They provide food, shelter, and nesting places for all sorts of birds, insects, and other water creatures.

Weather

Three things cause the weather: air, Sun, and water. Air is always on the move and makes the wind. The Sun gives warmth, and the water makes clouds, rain, snow, and hail. In some parts of the world the weather changes all the time. One day the sky may be sunny, the next it may be cloudy.

▽ This picture shows how the Earth uses its water over and over again. It is called the **water cycle**.

1 Every day, the Sun's heat turns water from seas and lakes into an invisible gas called water vapor.

2 As the air rises, it cools down and the water vapor turns into tiny drops of water or ice crystals.

3 Lots of drops of water join together to make clouds. The wind blows the clouds over the land.

4 Water in the clouds falls as rain, hail, sleet, or snow.

5 Rivers carry the water back to the sea.

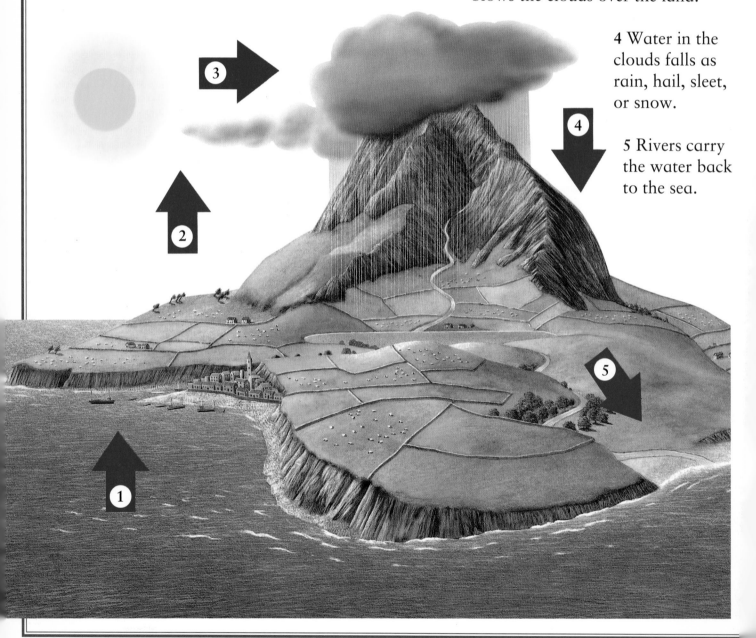

cirrus

stratus

cumulus

cumulonimbus

◁ There are different kinds of cloud. Fluffy clouds are called cumulus. Flat clouds are called stratus. Huge cumulonimbus clouds bring storms. Cirrus clouds are high up and wispy.

▷ Snowflakes are water drops that have frozen into ice crystals. No two snowflakes are ever the same.

▽ In very cold places, ice and snow often cover the land for most of the year.

△ Fog and mist are really clouds floating close to the ground. On roads, thick fog makes it difficult for drivers to see where they are going.

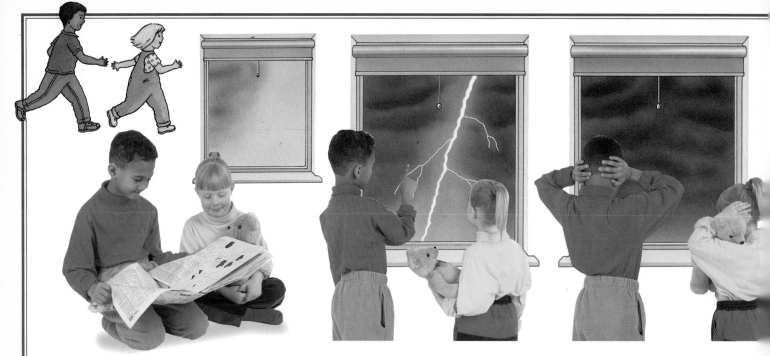

△ Thunderstorms start in big black thunderclouds that gather in the sky.

△ Electricity builds up inside the clouds. This causes big sparks of lightning.

△ When lightning flashes, it heats the air and makes a noise. This is thunder.

◁ A tornado is a spinning funnel of wind that races across the ground. As it spins, it sucks up rocks, trees, and even houses in its path.

△ Hailstones are frozen drops of rain. As they blow around inside a cloud, layers of ice form around them until they are heavy enough to fall.

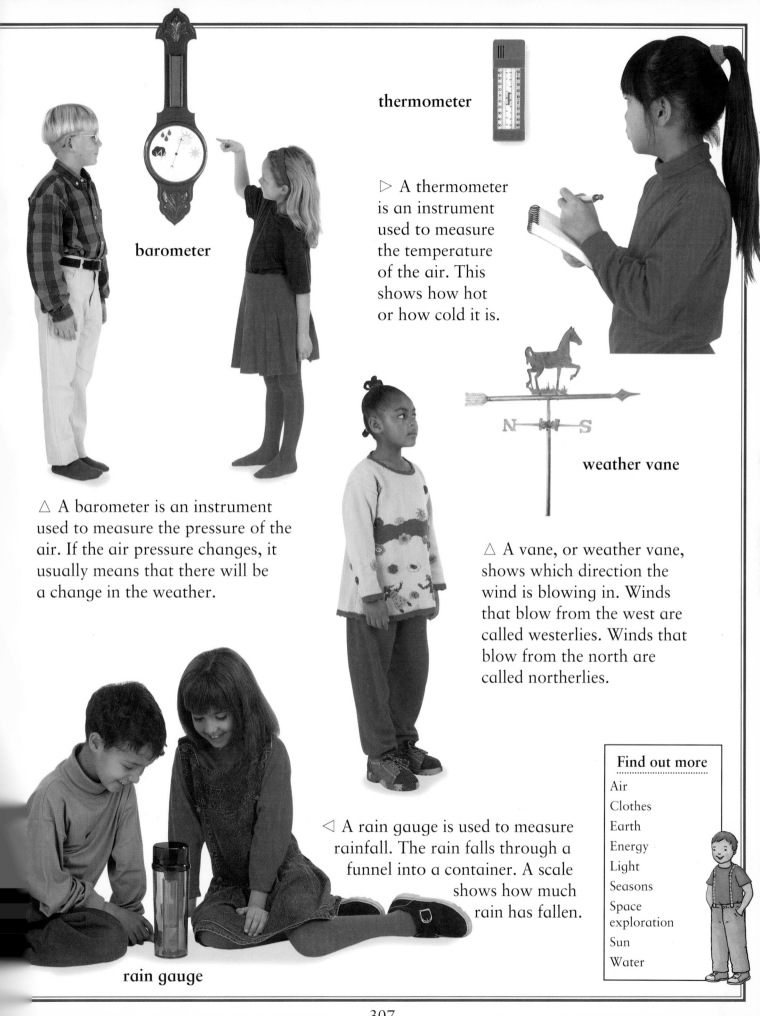

thermometer

barometer

▷ A thermometer is an instrument used to measure the temperature of the air. This shows how hot or how cold it is.

△ A barometer is an instrument used to measure the pressure of the air. If the air pressure changes, it usually means that there will be a change in the weather.

weather vane

△ A vane, or weather vane, shows which direction the wind is blowing in. Winds that blow from the west are called westerlies. Winds that blow from the north are called northerlies.

◁ A rain gauge is used to measure rainfall. The rain falls through a funnel into a container. A scale shows how much rain has fallen.

rain gauge

Find out more
Air
Clothes
Earth
Energy
Light
Seasons
Space exploration
Sun
Water

World

The sea covers most of the world. About one-third is covered by land. There are seven large areas of land, called continents. People have divided most of them into countries. Each country has its own name, its own money, and its own flag. There are about 190 countries in the world. Many different peoples live in each one.

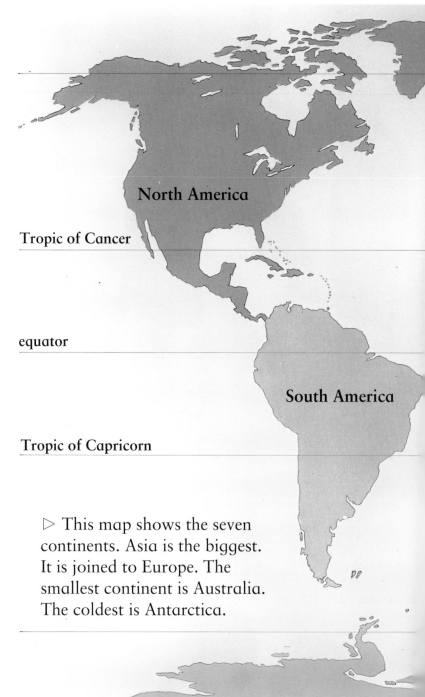

North America

Tropic of Cancer

equator

South America

Tropic of Capricorn

▽ On globes and maps an imaginary line, called the equator, divides the world in half. Countries nearest the equator are the hottest.

▷ This map shows the seven continents. Asia is the biggest. It is joined to Europe. The smallest continent is Australia. The coldest is Antarctica.

globe

▷ The world is round. To draw a flat map of it, mapmakers sometimes split its surface into several pieces, as if peeling an orange.

equator

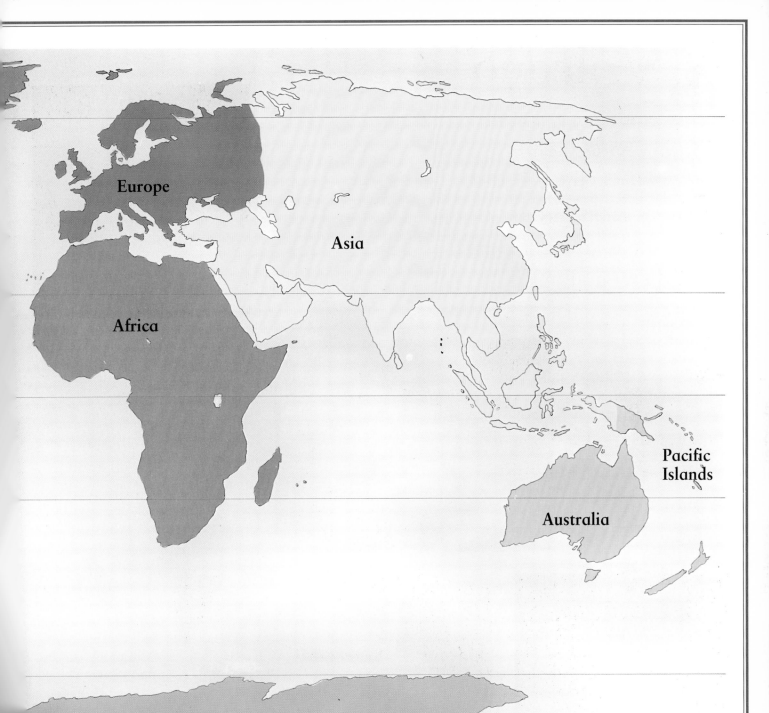

Europe

Asia

Africa

Pacific Islands

Australia

Antarctica

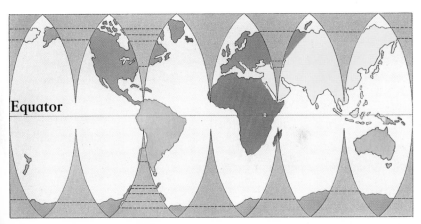

Equator

◁ The pieces
are laid flat
like this. But
this shows that
no flat map
can show how
the world has a
curved surface.

Find out more

Africa

Antarctica and
the Arctic

Asia

Australia and
the Pacific
islands

Europe

North America

South America

X rays

X rays are waves, similar to microwaves and light waves. They can pass right through flesh, but not through bones. X-ray photographs are used in hospitals, for example, to see if bones are broken. The bones show up light on a dark background.

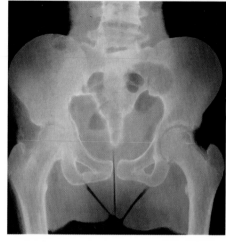

△ This is an X-ray picture of part of a child's back. It was taken to see if any bones were broken.

▷ This X-ray machine is being prepared to fire X rays down through the patient's leg. The X rays hit a sheet of film on the table beneath.

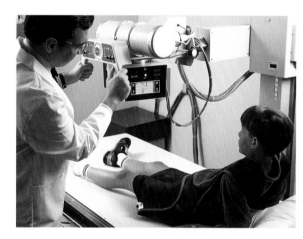

▽ X rays are used at airports to check people's baggage for dangerous items. As the bags go through the machine, the screen shows what is inside them.

One or two X rays will not harm you. Too many can be dangerous. People who work with them go behind a protective screen while the X rays are being taken.

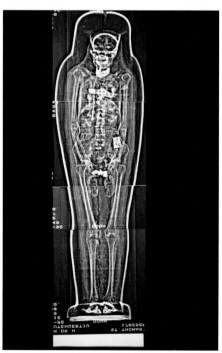

◁ In ancient Egypt, people wrapped dead bodies in cloth to preserve them. These bandaged bodies are called mummies. Modern scientists can use X rays to look inside the wrappings.

Find out more
Microwaves
Nuclear energy
Radio
Universe

Yak

Yaks are huge, shaggy oxen found on the high plains and mountains of Tibet. Their thick coats keep them warm in the bitter mountain winters. Some are wild, but most are kept as domestic animals.

△ The coats of domestic yaks (above) come in a range of colors from white to black. Wild yaks have long, silky black or brown coats and are bigger than domestic yaks.

▽ The yak was tamed over 2,000 years ago and gives the Tibetan people milk, meat, leather, wool, and transportation. Yaks are surefooted in rocky places and can survive in the harshest conditions.

◁ Wild yaks are nearly 6.5 feet high at the shoulder. The females and young live together in herds. The males prefer to live in smaller groups.

Find out more
Cow and Bull
Mammals

Year

A year is a length of time. Each year has 365 days. The days are divided into 12 months. Every four years, an extra day is added. This is called a leap year. Throughout the year, celebrations take place all over the world. Some are to remember things that have happened during a country's history or to celebrate the changing of the seasons.

△ All over the United States people celebrate Independence Day, on July 4, with parades, marching bands, picnics, pageants, and fireworks.

▷ Chinese New Year is celebrated between January and February. People dress up and set off noisy firecrackers in the street.

▽ Birthday parties are a popular way to celebrate the day someone was born on. Which day is your birthday?

Find out more
Babies
Moon
Seasons

The publisher would like to thank the following for contributing to the book:

Photographs

AKG Photo 149; Allsport USA 276 *r*, 277, 288 *cr*, *bl*; Andy Teare Photography 35, 36, 41, 92, 129 *t*, *b*, 144 *tl*, 211 *t*, 212, 215, 247, 261 *t*, 283, 294; Archiv für Kunst und Geschichte 26 *b*; © ARS, NY and DACS, London 1996 27 *b*; Bob Thomas Sports Photography 196 *tr*; Brian and Cherry Alexander 21 *bl*; Bridgeman Art Library 26 *l*, 27 *tr*, 64 *tr*, 286 *tr*; Bruce Coleman 9 *bl*, 166 *tl*, 183 *tr*, 285 *tr*; Cine Contact 271 *t*; Circa Photo Library 236 *l*; Colorific 146 *r*, 203 *l*, 235, 236 *t*; Dognall Worldwide 202; Eye of Science/Science Photo Library 188 *b*; Greg Evans International 149 *m*, 200, 276 *l*; IBM Eurocoor 72/73 *t*; Images 31 *t*, 203 *r*; Image Bank 132 *cl*; Image Colour Library 175 *tl*; Image Select 147 *r*, 148 *b*; Lawson Woods 30; Liam Muir 193; Lupe Cunha Pictures 32 *r*; Lyndon Parker 34, 54, 57, 65 *t*, 74 *t*, 76, 82, 86, 108, 129 *b*, 135, 136, 139, 144 *tr*, 150, 188 *t*, 214, 219, 228, 232, 248, 257, 260; Mary Evans Picture Library 120, 184 *cl*; NHPA 21 *t*; NHPL 29; Oxford Scientific Films 23, 25, 33, 43 *cr*, 50, 62, 65 *b*, 69, 74 *m*, 77, 87, 89, 90, 93, 100 *mr*, *ml*, 140 *m*, 154 *b*, 163, 173, 185, 192, 209, 211 *br*, 213, 224, 231, 244, 249, 250, 251, 255 *tl*, 261 *m*, 262, 275, 279 *t*, 311, 313; Panasonic 288 *bl*; Peugeot 37 *bc*; Planet Earth Pictures 11 *m*, 78, 95, 100 *t*, 140 *t*, 229, 300; RAC 116 *tl*; Renault UK Ltd 130 *bl*; Rex Features 189 *tl*, 230 *cl*; Robert Harding 32 *l*, 98 *t*, 101 *cl*, 103 *tr*, 132 *cr*, 174 *cl*; Ronald Grant 281 *b*, © 1996 Marvel Characters Inc. *m*; Science Photo Library 43 *cl*, 51 *bl*, 72 *tr*, 73 *tr*, 94, 167 *br*, 184 *br*, 186 *c*, 230 *bl*, 284 *tr*, 288 *cl*, 295, 310 *tr*, *br*; Sony 298 *bl*; Spectrum Colour Library 10, 11 *t*, 31 *b*, 107 *b*, 147 *t*, 148 *m*; Stephen Hughes/St.Thomas's Hospital 310 *bl*; Telegraph Colour Library 187 *b*, 237 *ml*, 299 *cr*; Thomas Neile/Hornby 98 *c*, *bl*; Tony Stone Associates 14, 152 *br*, 154 *ml*, 204 *c*, 255 *cb*, 267 *cb*, 268 *bl*, 269 *br*, 287 *cl*, 288 *tr*, 299 *tr*; TRIP 21 *m*, 237 *tr*; Zefa 107 *t*, 146 *l*, 177 *cr*, 187 *l*, 193, 197 *t*, 198, 206, 233 *b*, 271 *bl*, 305 *m*, *r*, 306, 310 *c*; Zefa/Ronald Grant Archive 298 *c*; All other commissioned photographs **Tim Ridley**.

Artists

Graham Allen, Hemesh Alles, Norman Arlott, Mike Atkinson, Craig Austin, Julian Baker, Bob Bampton, Julie Banyard, John Barber, Peter Barrett, Caroline Bernard, Richard Bonson, Robin Bouttell, Maggie Brand, Eric T Brudge, Peter Bull, John Butler, Robin Carter, Lynn Chadwick, Jim Channel, Kuo Kang Chen, Harry Clow, Dan Cole, Stephen Conlin, Rachel Conner, David Cook, Bob Corley, Peter Dennis, Maggie Downer, Sandra Doyle, Richard Draper, Brin Edwards, Michael Fisher, Cecelia Fitzsimons, Eugene Fleury, Roy Flooks, Wayne Ford, Chris Forsey, Rosamund Fowler, Mark Franklin, Andrew French, Terence Gabbey, Michael Gaffrey, Lee Gibbons (Wildlife Art Agency), Tony Gibbons, Mike Gillah, Peter Goodfellow, Ruby Green, Ray Greenway, Craig Greenwood, Peter Gregory, Ray Grinaway, Nick Hall, Darren Harvey, J Haysom, Tim Hayward (Bernard Thornton Artists), David Holmes, Steven Holmes, Adam Hook, Christa Hook, Steve Howes, Biz Hull, Mark Iley, Ian Jackson, Ron Jobson (Kathy Jakeman), Kevin Jones, BL Kearley, Roger Kent (Garden Studio), Deborah Kindred, Martin Knowelden, Mike Lacey, Stuart Lafford, Terence Lambert, R Lewington, Che'en Ling, Mick Loates, Bernard Long, (Temple Rogers), Andrew MacDonald, Kevin Maddison, Mainline Design, Alan Male (Linden Artists), Shirley Mallinson, Maltings Partnership, Janos Marffy, David Marshall (Simon Girling and Associates), Josephine Martin, S McAllinson, Angus McBride, Doreen McGuiness (Garden Studio), B McIntyre, G. Melhuish, Tony Morris, Maggie Mundy Illustrators Agency, Steve Noon, William Oliver, R. W. Orr, Oxford Illustrators, Nicki Palin, Alex Pang, Darren Pattenden, Bruce Pearson, Andie Peck, Bryan Poole, Jonathan Potter, Clive Pritchard, Sebastian Quigley (Linden Artists), Elizabeth Rice, J Rignall, Steve Roberts, Bernard Robinson, Eric Robson, G. Robson, Mike Roffe, Eric Rowe, Mike L. Rowe, Mike Saunders, Liz Sawyer, Peter David Scott, Brian Smith, Guy Smith (Mainline Design), Annabel Spencely, Clive Spong, Paul Stangroom, M. Stewart, Roger Stewart, Treve Tamblin, Myke Taylor (Garden Studios), Simon Tegg, Ian Thompson, Joan Thompson, Guy Troughton, Richard Ward, Ross Watton, T. K. Wayte, Wendy Webb, Lynne Wells, David Whatmore, Graham White, Wildlife Art Agency, Ann Winterbottom, David Wood, Dan Wright, David Wright